Figural Designs in Zuni Jewelry

TOSHIO SEI

Schiffer Publishing Ltd

4880 Lower Valley Road • Atglen, PA 19310

Library of Congress Control Number: 2013950216

Designed by RoS
Type set in Adobe Jenson/Gill Sans Std

ISBN: 978-0-7643-4558-6
Printed in China

Published by Schiffer Publishing, Ltd.
4880 Lower Valley Road
Atglen, PA 19310
Phone: (610) 593-1777; Fax: (610) 593-2002
E-mail: Info@schifferbooks.com

For our complete selection of fine books on this and related subjects, please visit our website at **www.schifferbooks.com**. You may also write for a free catalog.

This book may be purchased from the publisher. Please try your bookstore first.

We are always looking for people to write books on new and related subjects. If you have an idea for a book, please contact us at **proposals@schifferbooks.com**

Schiffer Publishing's titles are available at special discounts for bulk purchases for sales promotions or premiums. Special editions, including personalized covers, corporate imprints, and excerpts can be created in large quantities for special needs. For more information, contact the publisher.

Other Schiffer Books by the Author:
Knifewing and Rainbow Man in Zuni Jewelry
ISBN: 978-0-7643-3548-8 $24.99

Hopi Bird and Sun Face in Zuni Jewelry
ISBN: 978-0-7643-3882-3 $24.99

Kachinas and Ceremonial Dancers in Zuni Jewelry
ISBN: 978-0-7643-4167-0 $24.99

CONTENTS

ACKNOWLEDGMENTS

ACKNOWLEDGMENTS

Special thanks should first go to the Sheche family: Thelma, my closest friend in Zuni, her brother, Curtis Kucate, her son, Arden Kucate, and her daughter, Lorandina Sheche. They have accepted me as a family guest for more than ten years and introduced me to other artists such as Rita Edaakie, Bessie Vacit, Sarah Leekya, and Juana Homer. These artists further introduced me to their relatives such as Raphael Homer Jr., Anna Rita Homer, Raylan Edaakie, and Bradley Edaakie. When I first began to do this project, Leonard Martza helped me to identify artists who made certain older jewelry pieces I had owned. His elder sister, Genevieve Tucson, taught me who Harry Deutsawe was and what kind of pieces he made. This book owes a lot to these generous artists.

My old friends and potters, Milford and Randy Nahohai, told me where certain artists lived and drew me maps to find them. Without their help, I could not have visited and interviewed these artists. I always appreciated their hospitality and help.

After I published my first Zuni jewelry book, *Knifewing and Rainbow Man in Zuni Jewelry*, I became acquainted with Tom Kennedy, the director of the Zuni Tourism and Visitor Center. He helped me plan my collection show, book signing, and presentation surrounding my three books at the Visitor Center, where I met many wonderful Zuni people and artists including Dan Simplicio Jr., Roger Tsabetsaye, Marcus Peyketewa, and one of the grand-daughters of Arnold Cellicion.

A contributor to *Gallup Journey* and *Indian Trader*, Ernie Bulow, and I have become friends and helped each other to do field research on Zuni jewelry and artists. He introduced me to the daughters of Arnold and Neva Cellicion. Ernie's wife, Michelle G. Peina, a Zuni jeweler, has helped me to identify earlier unsigned pieces made by her father-in-law, Joe Zunie.

Lastly, without my wife Noriko's generous understanding of my passion for collecting, I could not compile my Zuni jewelry collection in this book. My daughter, Makiri, my son-in-law, Chad, and my son, Yuki, have helped me to compile this collection. Yuki helped me proofread my rough draft as well. Without their help, this book would not have become a reality.

INTRODUCTION

I have already published three Zuni jewelry books, which dealt with a combined six major motifs in Zuni jewelry: Knifewing and Rainbow Man, Hopi Bird and Sun Face, and Kachinas and Ceremonial Dancers. In this fourth book, I am going to deal with all remaining figural designs such as Butterfly, Dragonfly, Horse, Steer, wild animals, and so on. They are mainly created in the mosaic inlay or overlay style, but a few are done in the turquoise channel inlay style or carved nugget style.

Of these designs, Knifewing and Rainbow Man designs were created first, in the late 1920s, and then came Sun Face and Hopi Bird. These designs have been staples of Zuni jewelry ever since. As Kachina and Ceremonial Dancer designs are controversial, they were created later, mainly in the 1940s. At the same time, traditional carvings such as butterfly, dragonfly, steer head, and frog were set for rings, pins, and bolos.

The first literature which featured carved butterfly and dragonfly pins is the book by John Adair (1944, p. 192, plate 22). As it was published in 1944, they were made in the 1930s, by Teddy Weahkee, and set in silver by Okweene Neese (Adair, 1944, p. 149). Another earlier article which features the related designs in my book is in *Arizona Highways*, published in 1945. There is only one Butterfly pin made in the mosaic overlay style. It is perfectly designed and executed with a lot of dot inlay.

The August, 1952, issue of *Arizona Highways* features a wide variety of Zuni mosaic designs. In addition to Knifewing, Rainbow Man, and Butterfly, there are Sun Face, Hopi Bird, Rain Bird, Hopi Maiden, elk, donkey, horse, an Indian boy, and woman at her loom. In the late 1950s, Kachinas such as Long Horn, Long Hair and Eagle, basket dancer, and geometric designs appear in addition to Knifewing, Rainbow Man, Sun Face, Hopi Bird, horse, and steer (*Arizona Highways*, August, 1959, pp.9-11).

Another resource is the *C. G. Wallace Auction Catalogue* from the C. G. Wallace Collection of American Indian Art (Sotheby Parke Bernet, 1975). It includes 217 jewelry pieces related to the designs introduced in my book: butterfly; dragonfly; insects, such as fly and beetle; frog; tortoise; snake; bird; wild animals; horse; steer; foliate, such as flower and leaf; cross; arrow; human parts and figure; Rain Bird; cloud and rain; geometric and others. Of these eighteen designs, foliate has the most representation (thirty-six pieces). Geometric has the second most, with thirty-three pieces. Coming in third is butterfly

DESIGNS	1921-1930	1931-1940	1941-1950	1951-	UNIDENTIFIED	SUM (%)
Butterfly	3	4	5		13	25 (11.5)
Dragonfly	1	3	2			6 (2.8)
Insects	3				2	5 (2.3)
Frog	1	1			3	5 (2.3)
Turtle	1		1		6	8 (3.7)
Snake		1			6	7 (3.2)
Birds		2			22	24 (11.1)
Wild animals		3			18	21 (9.7)
Horse	4	2	1	1	1	9 (4.1)
Steer	4	1			3	8 (3.7)
Foliate		8			28	36 (16.6)
Cross	3	7	2			12 (5.5)
Arrow	1				6	7 (3.2)
Human					4	4 (1.8)
Rain Bird			1	1		2 (0.9)
Cloud/Rain	1				1	2 (0.9)
Geometric	2	4	1	1	25	33 (15.2)
Others					3	3 (1.4)
SUM	24 (11.1)	36 (16.6)	13 (6.0)	3 (1.4)	141 (65.0)	217 (100)

with twenty-five. There are twenty-four birds and twenty-one wild animals, ranking fourth and fifth, respectively. Although the years of make for 141 out of 217 pieces (65.0%) are unidentified, among the remaining 76 pieces, thirty-six pieces (16.6%) were made in the 1930s, twenty-four pieces (11.1%) were made in the 1920s, and thirteen pieces (6.0%) were made in the 1940s. Based on these data, these designs might have been conceived in the 1920s, and then became ordinary designs in Zuni jewelry in the 1930s. Here, we have to consider one condition: There is a possibility that a large portion of pieces in these designs falls into the category of carvings rather than mosaic works. Therefore, mosaic inlay or overlay pieces, which are the focus of this book, might have been made around ten years later than the C. G. Wallace Auction Catalogue suggests.

According to Dale Stuart King (1976), "C. L. Tanner noted that by the 1950's Life forms, particularly birds, were finding favor in the channel designs, and by the mid-1970's a favored style was the use of several colors of settings in a single channel piece" (p. 50).

In summary, the designs in my book may have been invented as early as the 1930s, and gradually become staple designs in Zuni jewelry in the 1940s and 1950s.

Arnold and Neva Cellicion's
and
Other Zuni Mosaic Artists'

BIOGRAPHIES

Arnold and Neva Cellicion

Arnold Cellicion (1928-1974) is the second oldest of the Cellicion brothers and married Neva Leekela Cellicion. He has been recognized as one of the great lapidaries of the craft. However, his work, specifically, was not known at the time my first book was published. During my book signing in Zuni from July 1 to 10, 2011, one of his granddaughters came to see my collection, closely examined ninety-nine pieces of my older Knifewing and Rainbow Man, and confirmed a couple of pieces as the work of Arnold and Neva Cellicion. These pieces are all similar to those confirmed as Teddy Weahkee's by C. G. Wallace. In general, pieces made by Teddy Weahkee and Arnold Cellicion are very similar, and, consequently, both are technically and aesthetically exceptional.

Recently, my friend and writer for *Gallup Journey* and *Indian Trader*, Ernie Bulow, wrote on Arnold and Neva Cellicion's Knifewing set (*Gallup Journey*, February 2012, pp. 20-21):

In a recent book, Japanese writer/collector Toshio Sei notes the similarity between his (that is, Mingos House) work and some pieces attributed to the great innovative artist Teddy Weahkee. He concludes that it certainly is a mystery, but leaves it at that.

In the same book, Sei notes that one of the four Cellicion brothers (all master jewelers along with their wives), the eldest, Arnold, doesn't have any identified existing work. Since Arnold's widow, Neva, is still alive it seemed logical to ask her. She—backed by two of her daughters—pointed to those same pieces that belong to Mingos or to Teddy Weahkee as their work.

Ernie asked her for some samples of their work as evidence, and Neva's daughter, Florence Lahaleon, provided him with a Knifewing set pasted on cardboard for photographing. He also discovered a Knifewing bracelet made by Arnold and Neva Cellicion and set by Neva's sister, Marrietta Soseeah, that was similar to Weahkee's work as well (*Gallup Journey*, March, 2012, pp. 20-21).

On July 3, 2012, I visited Neva's daughters, as Neva passed on at the end of June, 2012, and brought with me ten

Knifewing and Rainbow Man pieces, possibly by Arnold Cellicion or Teddy Weahkee, seeking their identification. I visited Florence Lahaleon first and showed her those ten pieces. She identified seven pieces as her parents', two as her uncle Oliver Cellicion's, and only one as probably Teddy's. I visited another daughter, Candeloria Cellicion, and showed the same pieces. The results were exactly same.

These seven Knifewing and Rainbow Man pieces are attributed to Arnold and Neva Cellicion by their daughters. I examined these again and compared them with the pieces found by Ernie Bulow. The result is as follows: In spite of their daughters' attribution, the only piece which should be attributed to Arnold and Neva Cellicion is the Knifewing bolo in the top left because of the straight lines in its kilt and wider face. For example, the Rainbow Man pin in the lower right has a leg shape that is not consistent with the Cellicions' work, and, therefore, could have been made by a different lapidary. As for the remaining five pieces, I would like to stick to the original attribution, that is, Teddy Weahkee or his close relatives.

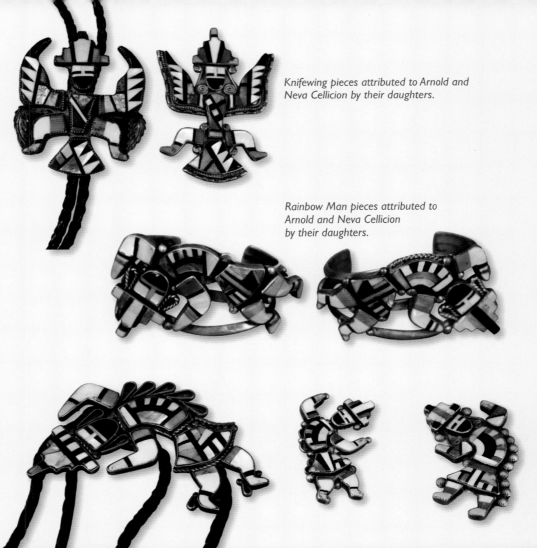

Knifewing pieces attributed to Arnold and Neva Cellicion by their daughters.

Rainbow Man pieces attributed to Arnold and Neva Cellicion by their daughters.

Knifewing pin made by Teddy Weahkee.

Knifewing pieces attributed to Oliver and Angela Cellicion.

These two Knifewing pieces are attributed to Oliver Cellicion, the oldest of the Cellicion brothers, by Arnold and Neva's daughters. We can see a clear similarity between Knifewing designs made by Oliver Cellicion and by Arnold and Neva Cellicion.

This is the only Knifewing which was not attributed to Arnold and Neva Cellicion by their daughters. As it is almost identical with the Knifewing pin in the *C. G. Wallace Auction Catalogue* (1975, 81, #443), it should be attributed to Teddy Weahkee. These six pieces attributed to Teddy Weahkee all have in common a curvilinear kilt. This feature is not incidental. They have fatter thighs and relatively narrower faces than Arnold and Neva's, as well.

According to Ernie Bulow, Neva is also from a famous jeweler family. Her sister is Marietta Soseeah and her brothers are Morris "Red" Leekela and Howard Leekela. Howard's son is Nicholas Leekela.

Virgil and Shirley Benn

Shirley Benn is a Hopi/Tewa and lived on the First Mesa, Polacca, till she was two years old. When her mother, Daisy Hooee Nampeyo, married Leo Poblano, Shirley came to live with her mother and father-in-law in Zuni. Her grandmother is Annie Nampeyo, and her great-grandmother, the famous Nampeyo. In the 1950s, she first made a large mosaic inlay piece which was a Hoop Dancer. She married Virgil Benn, and they began making animal motif jewelry together in the late 1960s. Shirley taught Andrea Lonjose Shirley, an ex-wife of her son, Bryson Pinto, how to make inlay jewelry.

Edward and Madeline Beyuka

Edward Beyuka (1921-2002) made jewelry for the first time in 1956. The authors of *Zuni: A Village of Silversmiths* (Ostler, and others, 1996, pp. 90-91) describe his learning process as follows:

Although he had watched his parents making jewelry while he was growing up, he didn't make any himself until 1956. He practiced in the evening while his family was at the Night Dances. Then he taught his wife Madeline to work with him—she did the inlay and he did the silverwork.

After their divorce, Edward did both silver and lapidary works. I met him on December 24, 2001. When I told Faye Quandelacy that I wanted to collect some Zuni mosaic jewelry, she took me to one of his sons at his trailer house. He was doing inlay work of a Buffalo Dancer for his father. I told him I would take it and ordered, through him, a Little Fire God from his father. While I relaxed in a room of the Inn at Halona, Edward Beyuka visited me without notice and asked me if I really wanted those two Kachina figures. I replied, "Yes, of course." Therefore, he made me a silver backing for the Little Fire God and two pairs of silver drums for bolo tips.

I visited Madeline Beyuka on December 28, 2009, and showed her my collection of their pieces. She showed me Edward's portrait, which was taken for the above-mentioned book. Madeline is a daughter of Simon Bica, a fetish carver. She told me where her sister, Angela Cellicion, lived. A potter, Quanita Kallestewa, is a sister of hers, as well.

Mary Jane Boone

Mary Jane Boone is a sister of Myra Tucson, one of the master artists in Zuni mosaic jewelry.

Della Casi (Casa Appa)

Della Casi (1889-1984) is known as the first female silversmith—as early as 1927—who had her own account at the C. G. Wallace trading post. She worked mainly in the beautiful nugget and cluster jewelry (Slaney, 1998, p. 27).

A lot of her jewelry was featured in the *C. G. Wallace Auction Catalogue* as well as *Zuni Jewelry* (Bassman, 2006, p. 13). The latter attributed to her a Hopi maiden pin. I believe this attribution is correct because, although it is similar to the same design made by Leo Poblano, his pieces have no pigment in their facial expressions, while the facial expression of Casi's piece was applied with black pigment. She made a Pueblo man figure in the traditional formal dress, and she might have made some turquoise channel works, as well.

Dexter Cellicion

After Dexter Cellicion (1931-1999) lost his first wife, Rosemary Wallace Cellicion, he married his second wife, Mary Ann, and made various Kachina jewelry in the 1950s and 1960s. After she passed on, he married Eva. We can see their Sun Face pins made in the mosaic inlay style, in the 1980s in *Zuni Jewelry* (Bassman and Bassman, 2006, p. 29). They are colorful examples of Sun Face jewelry.

Some of my informants attributed many older mosaic inlay pieces to Oliver Cellicion and Dexter Cellicion. Dexter Cellicion should be considered one of the master artists in Zuni jewelry history, although his work has been featured in only one book (Bassman and Bassman, 2006, pp. 29, 34). I met Eva Cellicion in December 2009 and interviewed her for a short time in front of her house. She seemed to know a little about his older pieces from the 1940s to the 1960s. When I asked one of Arnold and Neva Cellicion's daughters, "Who is the most wonderful artist of the four Cellicion Brothers?" she promptly answered, "Dexter."

Harry Deutsawe

I heard the name Harry Deutsawe (1912-1986) for the first time in March, 2009. When I visited an older active artist to order his old-style pieces, I showed him a Sun Face bolo that had not yet been decisively identified. It has been variously attributed to Leo Poblano or Lambert Homer Sr. The artist's elder sister, who lived with him, told me promptly it was made by Harry Deutsawe. He was their cousin and had lived with them since he was six years old. According to them, he had worked for C. G. Wallace as a lapidary. He was not a silversmith.

When Harry passed away in 1986, he left some unfinished pieces, which his cousin inherited. She showed them to me on September 20, 2010. They include two Sun Faces, two Rainbow Man pieces, one Knifewing, and a ranger buckle set, which have not been set on silver, but pasted on cardboard. There is a butterfly which has not been set on silver nor pasted on cardboard, and some other butterfly parts and a tip for a ranger buckle, as well. The lady's brother, the artist, set some of these pieces on silver for me.

Leekya Deyuse

Leekya Deyuse (1889-1966) is the single most famous jeweler in Zuni jewelry history. He was "originally a maker of large tab, nugget and disc bead necklaces in the old style" (Slaney, 1998, p. 27), and later became famous for his fetish carvings and fetish necklaces. As he was a turquoise worker, his lapidary works were mounted on the silver backings by various silversmiths including his son-in-law, Frank Vacit, and Dan Simplicio.

His son, Robert Leekya, has made wonderful nugget work jewelry with his wife, Bernice Ondelacy Leekya. She is a daughter of Doris and Warren Ondelacy and a sister of Alice Quam. Old Man Leekya's daughters, Alice, Elizabeth and Sarah, all made mosaic inlay jewelries. Alice and Sarah made fetish carvings, and Elizabeth made fine bead work, as well. Leekya Deyuse's wife, Juanita, made beadwork, too, and once did a gigantic horse for one of her grandchildren, who has since inherited it.

Juan de Dios

According to Slaney (1998, p. 33), Juan de Dios (1882-1944) produced Knifewings and crosses using the tufa cast technique. He learned the silver casting technique from a Navajo silversmith and taught it to his nephew, Dan Simplicio. Juan de Dios is one of the representative artists of the C. G. Wallace Collection as well. His name appears in Adair's list as Juan Deleosa (1944, p. 198).

He made some Knifewing figures, a cross with a Christ figure, steer heads, and channel inlay pieces set with turquoise.

Frank Dishta

Frank Dishta (1902-1954) is the creator of the Dishta Style channel inlay who worked for the C. G. Wallace Trading Post. According to Slaney, he was encouraged by Wallace to make channel work for the trading post around 1939 or 1940. She notes:

Dishta's channel designs are easy to recognize. His work was primarily geometric, with stones that were usually ground flush with the silver dividers. The stonework was often extremely minute, with circular stones as small as one millimeter in diameter arranged in geometric or flower-shaped cluster patterns. (Slaney, 1998, p.39)

His great-granddaughter, Mishelle Peina, told me Frank often encircled each cluster of channels set with tiny turquoise stones with a thin, twisted silver wire.

His wife, Pauline Dishta, made small earrings of snowflake design in the Dishta-style channel inlay.

Virgil Dishta Sr.

Virgil Dishta Sr. is a son of Frank Dishta and learned silversmithing in the 1930s, helping his parents make jewelry. He made jewelry full-time in the 1940s, when he married Margaret. His hallmark is "V Dishta" and was used first in the 1950s. They have several children including Virgil Dishta Jr., Duane Dishta, Vincent Dishta, and Joe Zunie's wife, Pauline Dishta.

Dennis and Nancy Edaakie

Dennis Edaakie (1931-2008) is a son of Merle Edaakie, the eldest of the four Edaakie brothers. Dennis and Nancy Edaakie worked mainly in silver overlay/mosaic inlay style. As pioneers of the use of this technique in the naturalistic birds, they established their own style and their place as master artists in Zuni Jewelry History. Their works have demanded high prices recently.

Merle Edaakie

Although collectors had agreed that Merle Edaakie, who was Dennis Edaakie's father, was one of the greatest mosaic overlay and inlay artists in Zuni Jewelry history, he had been known by name alone until my first Zuni jewelry book, *Knifewing and Rainbow Man in Zuni Jewelry*, was published in October, 2010.

His reputation is overwhelmingly positive. For example, according to Mark Bahti, "Merle made some of the finest inlay and mosaic work in Zuni" (2007, p. 44). In terms of Merle's specialty and professional affiliations, the authors of *Zuni: A Village of Silversmiths* say:

Dennis's father, Merle Edaakie, was a contemporary of Teddy Weahkee. He made the stone work for Knifewing and Rainbow Man figures for C. G. Wallace and the Vanderwagens, which they had set by Navajo silversmiths. (1996, p. 103)

Merle's name first appeared as "Merle Itaike" in the book by Adair (1944, p. 199), along with his younger brother, Lee Edaakie (1914-1984), or "Lee Itaike" in the book. He was the eldest of the Edaakie brothers; the others were Theodore (1911-1987) and Anthony (1927-1989). Although Theodore's Eagle Dancer was featured in the famous auction catalogue of the C. G. Wallace collection, along with many works by Lee, Merle's work neither appeared in the catalogue nor in any book/literature until the publication of my book (Sei, 2010, pp. 69-72).

Lee and Lita Edaakie

Lee Edaakie (1914-1984) is the second oldest of the Edaakie brothers. His name appears on the previously mentioned Adair's list. A lot of his jewelry in mosaic inlay, as well as the cluster work, are featured in the *C. G. Wallace Auction*

Catalogue and the *Arizona Highways: Hall of Fame Classics Edition*.

Lee Edaakie is listed as "Lee Itaike" in the list compiled by Adair in 1940 (1944, p. 199), and he utilizes a variety of styles, including cluster work and mosaic overlay.

Theodore (Ted) and Margaret Edaakie

Theodore Edaakie (1911-1987) is the third oldest of the Edaakie brothers. Although his name did not appear in Adair's list, his Eagle Dancer, owl, and roadrunner pins were included in the *C. G. Wallace Collection Auction Catalogue*. After he passed away, Margaret sold her lapidary works, which were mounted on silver backings by Leonard Martza, to the Pueblo Trading Post. Although Gregory Schaaf (2003, p. 147) describes Dennis Edaakie and Theodore Edaakie as brothers, Theodore is actually Dennis's uncle.

Anthony (Tony) and Rita Edaakie

Tony Edaakie (1927-1989) is the youngest of the Edaakie brothers. He is a jeweler as well as a painter and a wood carver of Kachina Figures, including Knifewing, Sun Kachina, and Moon Kachina. They put their hallmark, "Tony + Rita," on their pieces. Their son, Bradley, has made these wood carvings for the Zunis. Another son, Raylan, has made wonderful contemporary mosaic jewelry.

Tony and Rita raised Andrew Dewa, who lacked a caregiver in his childhood, and gave him a pattern of their Antelope Kachina design, after which his early Antelope Kachina pieces were modeled. Consequently, their art tradition is inherited by their sons, Bradley and Raylan, as well as by Andrew Dewa.

Ben Eustace

Ben Eustace is famous for his carved turquoise and silver leaves jewelry. He married a Cochiti lady and moved there.

Annie Quam Gasper

Annie Quam Gasper (1926-2001) was a daughter of Johnny Quam and a sister of Ellen Quam Quandelacy. She is the inventor of the abstract hummingbird design and spider web design (Slaney, 1998, p. 40). According to Gregory Schaaf, "She [is] one of the great masters who will long be remembered and honored" (2003, pp. 159-160).

Bernard Homer Sr. and Alice Leekya Homer

Bernard Homer is not a silversmith, but a lapidary, according to his daughter, Juana Homer. He had worked together with his brother, Lambert Homer Sr., at the C. G. Wallace Trading Post.

Bernard and his wife, Alice Leekya Homer, made channel inlay jewelry. From the 1970s, she stamped her hallmark "ALH" on her random pattern channel inlay work with turquoise, which stood for her first name, maiden name, and acquired family name. She is a daughter of Leekya Deyuse. All silver works were done by Alice Leekya

Homer. She did lapidary work and made some mosaic works, such as Rainbow Man and Hopi Bird, as well.

Lambert Homer Sr.

Lambert Homer Sr. (1917-1972) is no doubt one of the greatest mosaic overlay and channel inlay artists in Zuni jewelry history. His works have been consistently featured in many books, including the famous *C. G. Wallace Collection Auction Catalogue* (1975). This catalogue features numerous incredible works by Lambert Homer Sr. (although they are all attributed to his son, Lambert Homer Jr.), including a historic turquoise-inlaid belt made in collaboration with Roger Skeet. It may always remain a mystery, but in these cases, the name Lambert Homer Jr. might correctly mean Lambert Homer Sr.

Alonzo and Helen Hustito

Alonzo Hustito (1903-1987) might be the creator of the first Rainbow Man design for sale in any style of Zuni jewelry, as well as the first Knifewing for sale in mosaic overlay and inlay styles.

He worked with his wife, Helen Hustito (1924-1996), who was a niece of Theodore Kucate's Wife, Susie. As Alonzo was twenty-one years older than Helen, he might have made his jewelry in a completely different design and style before marriage, and changed them thereafter.

Horace Iule

Horace Iule (1901-1978) was one of the older Zuni silversmiths whose name appeared in the list of Zuni silversmiths compiled by Adair in 1940 (1944, pp. 198-199). This list is an invaluable source of information concerning Zuni lapidary artists and silversmiths in the 1930s.

He is represented in the C. G. Wallace collection as well. His silverwork was mainly in cast style set with turquoise. According to Adair (1944, pp. 137-142), he learned blacksmithing first at a school in Phoenix, Arizona, and learned silversmithing from his father after graduation in 1924. John Adair interviewed him intensively, observed the whole process of his work with silver, and described it in detail. According to Adair (1944, p. 139), Horace was the first silversmith to make Knifewing in silver, in 1928.

However, he might be more famous for his cross with turquoise set which was called the Iule Cross. He made other unique designs for pins and bolos as well.

On October 31, 2011, I visited his daughter, Lupe Iule Leekity (1941-), for the first time. I showed her two types of Iule Cross made by Horace. She told me there are only two versions of the Iule Cross, but they may be made in different sizes. I showed her a cast buckle with turquoise and coral set, which one of my informants attributed to Horace Iule. She confirmed it was made by her father in the late 1940s or early 1950s. The back and front of this buckle were made from one piece, which had been his old cast work method. Later, he cast only the front piece and soldered it on a silver plate. In addition, this buckle has a hand-made silver wire clasp instead of a factory-made swivel one.

Colleen Lamy

Juralita Lamy's daughters all carry on the tradition established by their mother. Colleen made an antelope design similar to the one made by her mother.

Dave and Johanna Lamy

Dave Lamy, the son of Juralita Lamy, made a wagon similar to his mother's. Dave and his wife, Johanna, signed their work "D & J Lamy Zuni."

Juralita Lamy

Juralita Lamy is famous for her Knifewing, Rainbow Man, covered wagon, and antelope jewelry. Her husband is William Lamy, and her daughters are Paulinis, Cindy, and Colleen Lamy.

Nicholas Leekela

Nicholas Leekela is a son of Howard and Katherine Leekela and a nephew of Morris "Red" Leekela, Neva Cellicion, and Marietta Soseeah.

Elvira Leekity (Kiyite)

Elvira Leekity made a marvelous butterfly pin in the 1990s, which was featured in the book *Zuni Jewelry* (Bassman, 1992, 56). Her butterfly design is extremely similar to the one made by Harry Deutsawe, both technically and design-wise. They both make butterflies in an overlay mosaic style, with silver parts being integral to the design, and they make similar butterfly forewings as well. However, a slight difference lies in the form of the forewings of their butterflies. While Harry's butterfly clearly consists of a heart shape in its forewings, the one made by Elvira shows some deformation, consisting of shapes reminiscent of raindrops.

Based on this fact, I guess there is a close relationship between Harry Deutsawe and Elvira Leekity. As she is a niece of Genevieve Tucson, and Harry Deutsawe is a cousin of Genevieve, whom he had lived with, Harry and Elvira are close relatives. According to Elvira, Harry taught her mother silver and lapidary works, and they were passed down to Elvira. Her family name is now Kiyite, since her husband passed away.

John Leekity (Gordon Leak)

"Very little is known about John Leekity (Gordon Leak), except that his mosaic work is superb" (Slaney, 1998, p. 32). According to an informant, his family name is Leekity. His favorite motifs were Knifewing and dragonfly, and, to a lesser degree, arrow. They are all inlaid in a jet background. His grandson is William Leekity, who is married to Nora.

Nora and William Leekity

Nora married William Leekity and began making jewelry in the 1940s. She is included in *Zuni: The Art and the People,* Vol. I (Bell, 1975, p.39).

Velma and Blake Lesansee

Velma (1925-2013) and Blake Lesansee (1921-1988) are famous for their owl design. However, they made dragonfly and cross designs in jewelry as well. Their daughter, Corraine Shack, and her husband, Bobby Shack, are famous for their Hopi bird/Thunderbird design, although they call it phoenix bird.

Jake Livingston

Jake Livingston is a son of Jake Haloo and a brother of Dolly Banteah, Nancy Laconsello, Lolita Natachu, and Rolanda Haloo. He first made traditional bird jewelry in the silver overlay/mosaic inlay style, but now is one of the master artists in contemporary innovative jewelry. He hallmarked his work, "J-I Livingston."

John and Cecilia Lucio

John Lucio (1919-1984) is very famous for his Eagle Dancer design. *Zuni: The Art and the People,* Vol. I (Bell, 1975, p. 20), explains that he began making jewelry in 1950, while *American Indian Jewelry I* (Schaaf, 2003) notes that, based on the *C. G. Wallace Auction Catalogue* (Sotheby Park Bernet, 1975), he had been active since the 1930s. According to the former book, he once was a member of the highly esteemed Zuni firefighters; therefore, he might have been a part-time jeweler before 1950. Based on my field research, other than his famous Eagle Dancer, he had made a variety of wonderful Kachina Jewelry including Hopi Snake Dancer, Buffalo Dancer, and Hoop Dancer. His wife, Cecilia, worked with him.

Jack Mahke

Jack Mahke is a son of Earle and Mae Mahke. His pieces are not featured in any book but *Zuni Jewelry* (Bassman, 1992, p. 14), although his career has lasted more than fifty years. His motifs are birds, animals, and flowers.

Leonard Martza

Leonard Martza is one of the artists who represents the famous C. G. Wallace collection. He is one of the oldest artists still active today. He had worked for C. G. Wallace's Trading Post from the 1950s, and he has worked for the Pueblo Trading Post in Zuni Pueblo thereafter. When I visited Zuni in the summer of 2003, he was providing silver work for pins and bracelets for mosaic overlay artists such as Margaret Edaakie and Betty Natachu.

Walter Nakatewa (Nahktewa)

Even though little is known about Walter Nakatewa (1894-1962), some information is available. He is one of the most represented artists of the C. G. Wallace collection. His eleven pieces were auctioned at the famous C. G. Wallace Collection auction held in 1975. The oldest pieces in the group were made in 1929, while half of them were from the late 1940s to the early 1950s. Therefore, he can be considered an outstanding artist even when compared to other greats of his time such as Leo Poblano, Lambert Homer Sr., and Frank Vacit.

He has three beautiful daughters, all of whom married famous artists and lived together with their father and mother, Rose Nakatewa. They are Agnes and Hugh Bowekaty, Esther and Bryant Waatsa Sr., and Mildred and Douglas Lesansee. They all made wonderful jewelry in the needle point style. Bryant Waatsa and Hugh Bowekaty, especially, have made Knifewing and Rainbow Man jewelry in this style. Their designs are very similar. Hugh and Bryant lived together in the same house and influenced one another. According to Hugh Bowekaty, the creator of the needle point style is Douglas Lesansee.

Amelio Nastacio

Amelio Nastacio was once the husband of Veronica Poblano. When they divorced, she left him the patterns of Mickey Mouse and Minnie Mouse, from which he made rings. Sullivan Shebola is his friend, and made similar Mickey Mouse and Minnie Mouse jewelry.

Betty and Gillerimo (Yelmo) Natachu

Betty Natachu (1933-) has made mosaic jewelry since she was eighteen years old. Since she was not a silversmith, her husband, Gillerimo Natachu, took care of the silver work, while Betty specialized in lapidary work. After her husband passed on, she started to sell her lapidary work without a silver backing to galleries. His first name was known as Yelmo among Zuni people and Native American artists.

Their Knifewing bracelet appeared in a book for the first time (Schiffer, *Turquoise Jewelry*, 1990, p. 20). It is a Knifewing bracelet in the mosaic overlay style that probably measures only two inches tall.

Considering its smaller size, her lapidary skill is well beyond our comprehension. She is one of the best miniature mosaic lapidaries of her time. Even more impressive was the fact that she had made her pieces with a hand grinder till 1990, when the grinder was broken. There was no part to replace the broken piece with, so she has used a motor grinder ever since. With this in mind, her pre-1990 lapidary skills are impressive enough, but her post-1990 skills have seemed to improve even more with the help of the motor grinder.

Sarah Neese

Sarah Neese is a daughter of Okweene Neese, and made carved leaf jewelry, which is smaller but similar to that made by the Old Man Leekya.

Doris and Warren Ondelacy

The cluster work of Doris (1902-2000) and Warren (1898-1980) Ondelacy is prominently featured in the famous C. G. Wallace collection. Doris was a younger sister of Theodore Kucate, and, therefore, an aunt of the famous fetish carver Thelma Sheche. Doris and Warren used their hallmark, "D. & W." After Warren passed on, Doris used her own hallmark: "D." Doris taught Thelma how to make a cluster work squash blossom necklace, which Thelma gave to her mother.

Henry Owelicio

One day in November, I noticed Thelma Sheche wore a turquoise channel inlay butterfly pin on her blouse. As it looked so different and unique, I asked her who made the pin. She answered, Henry Owelicio had made it. This was the first time I heard his name.

Later in the evening, I asked Thelma Sheche and her daughter, Lorandina Sheche, who Henry Owelicio was. They told me Henry Owelicio (1922-2007) was a close relative of Theodore Kucate and Helen Hustito, and they lived close to each other. Lorandina showed me two turquoise channel inlay dragonfly pins and told me the following story: Henry was very pleased that his clan-niece, Ilka Sheche, Theodore's great grand-daughter, worked for the navy. Just before he passed away in 2007, when Ilka had her second baby girl, Henry presented each of her two daughters with a beautiful turquoise channel inlay dragonfly pin.

Quincy Peynetsa

Little is known about Quincy Peynetsa (1943-1982) except that he made some wonderful Kachina jewelry in the silver overlay/mosaic inlay style. One of my collector friends in Texas sent me a photo of a Shalako bolo and mentioned Peynetsa as the probable artist. It reminded me of the work of Frank Vacit, but one of Frank's daughters denied it was her father's work. I have searched for Quincy Peynetsa in various reference books. However, I could not find any information about him. Some gallery home pages mention his name as the probable artist for some jewelry based on the hallmarks: QDP.

Most older Zuni artists do not know his name except for a few middle-aged artists. Some said his name might be Quintus Peynetsa or Quincy Panteah. Nevertheless, he existed, that is for sure, and made marvelous mosaic jewelry in the silver overlay/mosaic inlay style.

Quincy Peynetsa had a tragic premature death in 1982. He signed some of his pieces, but many pieces remained unsigned. He made Kachina jewelry including Mudhead and Shalako which are similar to the ones Frank Vacit made. His skills were outstanding. However, he died before developing his own style of art and could not achieve artistic virtuosity.

Ida Vacit Poblano

Ida Vacit (1925-1987) married Leo Poblano in 1947, and they used to live where their daughter, Veronica Poblano, founded her own gallery: Galleria Poblano in Zuni.

After Leo died tragically while firefighting in California, Ida Vacit Poblano completed many of her husband's unfinished pieces (Slaney, 1998, P. 28). As she was not a silversmith, but a lapidary, she sold her mosaic pieces without silver backings to galleries such as C. G. Wallace, John Kennedy, Tobe Turpen, and others (Harmsen, 1988, p. 4). Sometimes, Navajo silversmiths, such as Ike Wilson and Mary Morgan, did the silver work for her mosaic overlay pieces, so, these finished pieces inevitably exhibited a Navajo flavor. As for her mosaic lapidary work, all of her pieces have an authentic Zuni taste. She is most famous for Zuni Kachina figures from the Harmsen Collection, which are joint works with Navajo silversmith Mary Morgan.

Leo Poblano

Leo Poblano (1905-1959) is without doubt one of the greatest artists in Zuni jewelry history. He is a nephew of Teddy Weahkee. In 1939, he married a Hopi/ Tewa potter, Daisy Hooee Nampeyo, granddaughter of the single most famous Hopi/Tewa potter: Nampeyo. Leo taught Daisy Zuni lapidary work, and she taught him three-dimensional relief techniques, which she had learned at L'Ecole des Beau Arts in Paris in 1929 (Slaney, 1998, p. 28). They divorced in the early 1940s. One of the contemporary representative mosaic lapidaries, Shirley Benn, is Daisy's daughter from her earlier marriage.

Leo Poblano then married Ida Vacit in 1947. They had four children including Veronica Poblano, Charlotte Eustace, and Faye Lonjose, all of whom are marvelous jewelers. He died tragically in 1959 while firefighting in California.

He did not convert to an electric grinder until the late 1950s (Slaney, 1998, p. 28), although it was introduced to Zuni in 1954. The faces of his ceremonial dancers and Kachinas are carved in the relief techniques without black pigment. It could be considered his signature.

Veronica Poblano

Veronica Poblano (1951-) is a daughter of Leo Poblano and Ida Vacit Poblano. She was eight years old when her father passed on. Madeline and Edward Beyuka, whose house is close to Veronica's, helped her a great deal in learning silver and lapidary works. She told Kari Chalker (2004, p. 186): "When I was maybe thirteen years old, my neighbors Madeline and Edward Beyuka introduced me to silversmithing. I used to go visit and watch them work while they did their lapidary. They did a lot of mosaic inlay work, creating all kinds of Zuni dancers and Katsina figures."

In her mid-twenties, she was inducted into the Arizona Highways Hall of Fame Classics under her married name, Veronica Nastacio (*Arizona Highways*, August, 1974, p. 44). Her pieces from those days are Disney characters, such as Mickey Mouse and Minnie Mouse. She carved those figures in the three-dimensional and cubic manner. Her lapidary skills were far beyond the level of most in those days and continue to outshine her would-be lapidary peers today; although we may encounter some Disney characters being made in mosaic work presently, they do not exceed Victoria's lapidary skill level in her prime.

After working as a beautician in California, she came home to Zuni and worked as a contemporary creative jewelry designer and lapidary. She has been recognized as one of the representative artists in this area ever since.

Deann Qualo

Deann Qualo is a daughter of Juan Qualo Jr. and Marie Qualo. Like her parents, her specialty is also quail.

Effie Qualo

Effie Qualo married Elliot Qualo. Her Ram ring is in *Zuni Jewelry* by Theda and Michael Bassman (p. 14, 1992).

Elliot Qualo

Elliot Qualo (1930-1974) was the younger brother of Juan Qualo Jr. Their parents were Juan Qualo Sr. and Myra Acque Qualo. Elliot is included in the *Arizona Highways: Hall of Fame Classics Edition* (August 1974, pp. 32, 44), even though he was relatively young compared to his contemporaries, including Ed Beyuka, Porfilio Sheyka, Dennis Edaakie, and Lee and Mary Weebothee. *Arizona Highways* magazine featured his Apache Gahn Dancer set for men and a Ram's Head pin. He was one of the master artists of the 1970s.

June Qualo

June Qualo (1948-) is a daughter of Myra Tsipa Qualo. Her cross pendant and earrings in the snake eye style are featured on the same page in *Who's Who in Zuni Jewelry* by Gordon Levy (p. 58, 1980).

Marie Qualo

According to *Zuni: The Art and the People*, Vol. 1 (Bell, 1975, p. 13), Marie Qualo had a twenty-five-year-long career as a jewelry artist. So, she began the art around 1950. Her specialty was a beautiful Sun Face with a small fan-shaped mouth and a complicated forehead design. An informant of mine told me her first name was Maria, which sounds Spanish.

Myra Tsipa Qualo

Myra Tsipa Qualo (1913-2008) married Juan Qualo Sr. Their daughters are May Qualo and June Qualo. She has another daughter from another marriage, Lorraine Nastacio, who married Juan Coonsis. Lorraine and Juan Coonsis's son is Harlan Coonsis. Myra Tsipa Qualo made her first jewelry in 1937 when she was twenty-four years old. She was a self-taught silversmith and lapidary.

Ellen Quam Quandelacy

Ellen Quam Quandelacy (1924-2002) is a daughter of Johnny Quam and a sister of Annie Quam Gasper. Although she became famous for her horse fetishes, she and her sister, Annie Quam Gasper, made wonderful channel inlay jewelry as well. Their works are very difficult to distinguish from each other. Her jewelry pieces are featured in *Zuni: The Art and the People*, Vol. 2 (Bell and others, 1976, p. 44).

Corraine Lesansee Shack

Corraine Shack is a daughter of Blake and Velma Lesansee and the wife of Bobby Shack. The couple are famous for their Phoenix bird/Thunderbird and hummingbird jewelry.

Thomasine Shack

Thomasine Shack is the mother of Bobby Shack and is included in *Zuni: The Art and the People*, Vol. 1 (Bell, 1975, pp. 34-35). The potter Milford Nahohai classified her work as exceptional (Ostler and others, 1996, p. 128).

Porfilio and Ann Sheyka

Porfilio (1938-1982) and Ann (1943-) Sheyka made a variety of birds, including quail bird, owl, and eagle, as well as rabbit and frog. Porfilio makes Eagle Kachina as well, which appears in the *Arizona Highways: Hall of Fame Classics Edition* (1974, p. 32) and in *Ray Manley's Collecting Southwestern Indian Arts & Crafts* (1975, p. 24).

Dan Simplicio

Dan Simplicio (1917-1969) was the creator of the nugget work style and one of the greatest artists in Zuni jewelry history, which makes use of naturally shaped turquoise nuggets and coral twigs, along with filed and stamped silver leaves and stamped silver drops.

His mother was the youngest sister of Juan de Dios. According to King (1976, p. 60), "It was Juan de Dios who helped to encourage Dan to become a good craftsman. He taught Dan to melt silver coins and to make leaves of different sizes. This was in the middle '20s."

After Dan established his nugget work style, he taught silversmithing to his brothers, Chauncy Simplicio and Mike Simplicio, and his nephew, Juan Calavaza, husband of Effie Calavaza.

Although he was most famous for his nugget style jewelry, he did mosaic inlay work as well. His Knifewing brooch from the late 1920s or early 1930s and Knifewing earrings from the 1930s or 1940s appear in *Southwest Silver Jewelry* (Baxter, 2001, pp. 111, 132). They are all in the Lynn D. Trusdell collection. It is extremely rare for Zuni pieces to be attributed to a specific artist.

Dan Simplicio Jr. recalled his late parents, Dan Sr. and Esther (1925-1971), and their silversmithing situation in the 1960s:

> He worked for a trading company in Gallup, and she stayed home…. He would do the silverwork and leave it behind, and go out to work the next day. She would set the stones and polish them as well, so by the time he got back, those would be finished and he could start on another set. (Gomez, 2005, p. 35.)

Dan Simplicio Sr. worked with Navajo silversmiths in Gallup, and this unique situation led to an exchange of previously foreign ideas and techniques. "They were bouncing ideas off each other, and I think they produced some of the greatest pieces of that time," Dan Simplicio Jr. said, referring to the 1960s. "A whole different style came out of that, and they were some of the pioneers."

Isabel and Chauncy Simplicio

Chauncy Simplicio is a younger brother of Dan Simplicio. Dan taught his brothers, Mike and Chauncy, how to make jewelry. Isabel and Chauncey's specialty is horse head, which is similar to Dan's. It is included in *Zuni: The Art and the People*, Vol. 1 (Bell, 1975. p. 60).

Lena Paywa Theslakia

Lena Paywa Theslakia is a daughter of Bowman Paywa. She is a potter and a jeweler, and works for the Zuni Visitor and Arts Center as a cultural interpreter.

David Tsikewa

David Tsikewa is better known for his fetishes and fetish necklaces than for his mosaic overlay jewelry. He was active from the late 1930s to 1970. Before he married Mary, daughter of Teddy Weahkee, he was a mosaic overlay jeweler. After their marriage, David and Mary seemed to concentrate more on fetish and fetish necklaces, and they became two of the best fetish carvers ever, following only Leekya Deyuse, Teddy Weahkee, and Leo Poblano. According to McManis (2003, p. 21), he learned silversmithing from Horace Iule in or around 1937, and his name appears as David Siaekewa in Adair's list (1944, p. 199).

Myra and Lee Tucson

Myra Tucson is an accomplished jeweler who represented Zuni artists in the 1960s, specifically at the "Southwest Indian Arts II" exhibition, held at California Palace of the Legion of Honor, San Francisco, in 1965, where she showed her art along with an innovative Navajo artist, Kenneth Begay (Schaaf, 2003, p. 314).

As many pieces were attributed to her by my informants, she could be considered, by older artists at the present time, one of the most recognized artists. Her former husband is Homer Vacit.

Frank and Elizabeth Leekya Vacit

Frank Vacit (1915-1999) is one of the most well-represented artists of the famous C. G. Wallace Collection. He married one of Leekya Deyuse's daughters, Elizabeth Leekya (1919-2005), who was a lapidary as well as a bead work artist. His younger brother, Homer Vacit, is a wonderful mosaic jewelry artist as well. Frank has a son, Gary Vacit, and three daughters, including Bessie and Jovanna. They are all skilled lapidaries. A book (Schaaf, 2003, p. 257) describes Leo Poblano's last wife, Ida Vacit Poblano, as a niece of Frank Vacit, and another book (Slaney, 1998, P. 42) as his daughter. According to one of her daughters, Ida is not Frank's daughter.

One of his daughters told me that his friend in California presented him with a gigantic sea turtle shell in the 1950s,

and, thereafter, her father used it to make backgrounds for mosaic figures instead of overlaid silver one.

Homer and Myra Vacit

Homer Vacit is a younger brother of Frank Vacit. His former wife was Myra, who later married Lee Tucson.

Homer's name had come up in neither my earlier field nor literature research. However, I showed a photocopy of an older Rainbow Man necklace in *Arizona Highways* (August 1952, p. 10) to an older informant who told me it was made by Homer Vacit. It was the first time I had heard his name. Since then, his name has come up more often among my informants. He was an excellent lapidary who could compete with any of the most famous Zuni artists.

Gary and Paulinis Mae Vacit

Gary Vacit, the oldest son of Frank Vacit, married Paulinis Mae Lamy, a daughter of Juralita Lamy. I used to wonder why the Knifewing and Rainbow Man designs made by Gary Vacit and Juralita Lamy looked

so similar. As soon as I discovered their relationship, the mystery was solved.

Winnie Wallace

Winnie Wallace is a sister of Rosemary Wallace Cellicion and made wonderful butterfly jewelry in the mosaic overlay style. She should be remembered as one of the great master artists in Zuni jewelry history.

Teddy Weahkee

If I were asked to name the three greatest artists in Zuni art history, I would pick Leekya Deyuse, Leo Poblano, and Teddy Weahkee. No one will object to my choices.

Weahkee is a mosaic overlay artist as well as a three-dimensional carver of fetishes and small sculptures, not to mention a two-dimensional painter. Although his name did not appear in the list of Zuni Silversmiths compiled by Adair, two of his turquoise dragonflies mounted on silver-backings by a Navajo silversmith were featured in the Adair book (1944, p. 149). A lot of his pieces are featured in the *C. G. Wallace Auction Catalogue*, including mosaic jewelries and stone carvings.

His nephew is Leo Poblano, son of Teddy's sister Katie Moote (McManis, 2003, pp. 17-19). His son-in-law, David Tsikewa, is married to his daughter, Mary Weahkee. She and her sister, Edna Weahkee Leki, are both wonderful fetish carvers as well.

Tom Weahkee

Tom Weahkee is a brother of Teddy Weahkee. Adair describes Tom as one of the best turquoise workers in the pueblo (1944, p. 140). He is also included in *Zuni: The Art and the People*, Vol. 1 (Bell, 1975, p. 42).

Dorothy and Bruce Zunie

Dorothy and Bruce (1931-1971) Zunie made marvelous Kachina Jewelry including Side Horn Kachina (Sotheby Parke Bernet, 1975, p.4), Sword Swallower, Eagle Kachina (Ostler and others, 1996, pp. 84-85), and Ram Kachina (King, 1976, p. 176). Based on the evaluations of these works, it's safe to say Bruce is one of the best mosaic jewelers in Zuni jewelry history. He is a cousin of brothers Joe Zunie, Lincoln Zunie, and William Zunie.

Joe Zunie and Pauline Dishta

Joe Zunie and his brothers, William and Lincoln, are sons of Willie Zunie. After Pauline Dishta married Joe, they worked together to create various motifs such as wonderful ceremonial dancers, domesticated animals like horses and cows, wild animals such as Ram, antelope and deer, and even Carp. They added etchings on their pieces which make them look realistic. Pauline is a granddaughter of Frank Dishta and the mother of Michelle Peina.

Lincoln and Helen Zunie

Lincoln Zunie is still active, although his wife, Helen Zunie, has passed on. He has made Eagle Dancer, covered wagon, ox, and horse. I got a covered wagon bolo directly from him in June, 2010.

Butterflies, Dragonflies, Frogs *and* Others

In this chapter, I am going to deal with designs such as Butterflies, dragonflies, Bees, Frogs and turtles.

1 *Butterflies*

We can observe many butterfly pieces in Zuni jewelry, whereas we can only find a few butterfly carvings in Zuni fetish. As I noted earlier, the C. G. Wallace Auction Catalogue *features twenty-five butterfly pieces (11.5%), and twelve of them are believed to be made between the 1920s and 1940s. Leekya Deyuse, Teddy Weahkee, Juan de Dios, Lee Edaakie, and Annie Quam Gasper claim two each while Jerry Watson, John Gordon Leekity, Leo Poblano, Della Casi, Lambert Homer, and Dan Simplicio each have one. All of the above are master artists.*

On the other hand, Kent McManis's introductory fetish book features no butterfly fetish, although some relief carving type jewelry pieces are included among these twenty-five pieces in the C. G. Wallace Auction Catalogue. Why does this discrepancy occur? It is probably because jewelers in the first half of the twentieth century had to adjust to the outside demand of white traders and customers, while the fetish carvers in the last quarter of the century had no such need. Instead, by that time, outside customers were seeking out the authentic Zuni fetishes made for Zuni purposes. Therefore, Zuni carvers sometimes have to declare that the carved butterfly is not a true fetish but a mere stone carving.

Butterfly pin, mosaic overlay, Lambert Homer Sr., silver work by a silversmith for Kennedy, no hallmark, 1950s, 3.40" x 1.87", $1000–1500.

Butterfly pin, mosaic overlay, Alonzo Hustito, no hallmark, 1950s–60s, 2.89" x 1.72", $800–1200.

Butterfly pin, mosaic overlay, Ida Vacit Poblano, no hallmark, 1950s–60s, 2.15" x 2.18", $800–1200.

In the 1950s, Lambert Homer Sr. made this butterfly pin, set by a silversmith at John Kennedy's Gallup Indian Trading Company, in the mosaic overlay style. It has characteristic stamp work on its antennae and both sets of wings. It measures 1.87 inches tall and consists of green turquoise, orange spiny oyster, iridescent abalone, white mother of pearl, and black jet. Mute colors together with intricate silver work make this pin a one-of-a-kind piece of jewelry.

Alonzo Hustito made this butterfly pin in the mosaic overlay style, in the 1950s or 1960s. Its stamps on both sides of the upper wings are very similar to the last one, by Lambert Homer Sr. These two might be set by the same silversmith. However, the butterfly patterns of these two lapidary works are apparently different in every way except for their central bodies. This pin measures 1.72 inches tall and consists of green turquoise, orange spiny oyster, white clam shell and black jet.

This is a butterfly pin made by Ida Vacit Poblano in the mosaic overlay style, in the 1950s or 1960s. As it lacks red and orange, it does not look colorful. The turquoise parts in its body and wings are the same shade of green, but different from the blue in its eyes. Therefore, Ida apparently did her lapidary work without eyes, and then the silversmith added them when he/she set Ida's lapidary work on silver backing. It measures 2.18 inches tall and consists of green turquoise, blue turquoise, white mother of pearl, and black jet.

Butterfly pin, mosaic overlay, Ida and Leo Poblano, no hallmark, 1950s, 2.04" x 1.70", $1600–2400.

Ida Vacit and Leo Poblano made this butterfly pin, in the mosaic overlay style, in the 1950s. The lapidary work is extremely well-done. In addition to sixteen inlaid dots, black and white parts in the upper wings fit into each other very well even though their contact lines are not straight, and very thin black and white parts are sandwiched between turquoise and spiny oyster parts in its body. While the body is very colorful, the wings are colorless. It measures 1.70 inches tall and consists of green turquoise, orange spiny oyster, white mother of pearl, and black jet.

Butterfly bolo, nugget work, Horace Iule, no hallmark, 1940s–50s, 1.684" x 1.69", $1000–1500.

In the 1950s, Horace Iule made this butterfly bolo, in the nugget work style. When I first saw it, I attributed it to John Lucio. However, my Zuni friend attributed it to Horace Iule. Then, I saw Lupe Iule Leekity at her home and asked if it was her father's work. She confirmed promptly that it was and that it resembled butterfly. Once she confirmed it was Horace Iule's work, I noticed the lapidary work was his, and, at the same time, that it is almost identical to Lupe Iule Leekity's. This piece is unique for his work in that it is not done in the tufa cast style. Its basal silver plate is cut out, stamped silver drops and strings are welded onto it, and five turquoise cabochons are set with saw-tooth bezels. It measures 1.69 inches tall. Matching tips enhance its attractiveness.

Butterfly ranger belt set, mosaic inlay, Myra and Homer Vacit, no hallmark, 1940s–50s, 1.78" x 1.86" for buckle, $1000–1500.

Butterfly pin, mosaic overlay, Leonard Martza, no hallmark, 1970s–80s, 2.87" x 2.52", $1000–1500.

Butterfly pin/pendant, nugget work, Doris and Warren Ondelacy, D. & W., 1960s–70s, 3.29" x 2.47", $1200–1800.

This is a butterfly ranger belt set made by Myra and Homer Vacit in the mosaic inlay style in the 1940s or 1950s. We can easily notice one butterfly in the buckle and the end tip. We can also notice some symbolic butterfly design in two keepers. This lapidary work is well-designed and well-executed far beyond our expectations. The buckle measures 1.86 inches tall, and the set consists of blue/green turquoise, orange spiny oyster, white mother of pearl, and black jet.

Leonard Martza made this butterfly pin/pendant in the mosaic overlay style in the 1970s or 1980s. It has six inlaid dots on black and white parts in its wings. Four thin black strips of jet divide outer and inner parts of the wings. In addition, its body also has six thin black and white parts sandwiched between turquoise, mother of pearl, and spiny oyster. This pin measures 2.52 inches tall and consists of green turquoise, orange spiny oyster, iridescent abalone, white mother of pearl, and black jet.

In the 1960s or 1970s, Doris and Warren Ondelacy made this butterfly pin, in the nugget work style. It has beautiful Lone Mountain turquoise cabochons, just like their cluster work jewelry from this era. In 2011, Lorraine Waatsa, one of their granddaughters, told me Doris and Warren used to make this kind of jewelry. Then, in the spring of 2012, I acquired this. One of Lorraine's sisters still makes similar jewelry. It measures 2.47 inches tall.

This is a butterfly bolo made by Thomasine Shack in the mosaic overlay style in the 1950s. She was featured in *Zuni: Art and the People*, Vol. I (Bell, 1975, pp. 34-35). However, her butterfly necklace design in the book is totally different from this one. On the other hand, several years ago, I noticed a smaller version of this butterfly design in the same silver work in *Zuni Jewelry* (Bassman, 1992, p. 13).

One evening in April, 2012, I was invited to dinner at Corraine and Bobby Shack's by their son, Daryl Shack. After dinner, I showed them the collection album for my fourth book. As soon as Bobby saw this bolo and the following four smaller pieces, he confirmed they were his mother's. As far as I could tell, her older butterfly pieces have in common three stamped silver drops over their bodies, and thin strips of parts can always be seen even if they are tiny, like the following pieces.

This bolo has two W-shaped silver wire clasps on its back. It measures 2.14 inches tall and consists of green turquoise, orange spiny oyster, white mother of pearl, and black jet.

Butterfly pendant, mosaic overlay, Thomasine Shack, no hallmark, 1950s, 0.87" x 1.35", $300–450.

Soon after I came home from my stay in Zuni in April, 2012, I found this mosaic overlay butterfly pendant, made by Thomasine Shack in the 1950s. Even if this butterfly design is not exactly the same as the bigger and smaller versions of her butterfly design, this is undoubtedly her piece. The triangular set of three stamped silver drops over its body is consistent with Thomasine's style, and the wing patterns are similar to those on the bigger and smaller versions, even if on this piece they are deformed a little bit. It measures 1.35 inches tall and consists of blue/green turquoise, orange spiny oyster, iridescent abalone, and black jet.

Butterfly pin, mosaic overlay, Thomasine Shack, no hallmark, 1950s, 0.82" x 0.83", $100–150.

Butterfly earrings, mosaic overlay, Thomasine Shack, no hallmark, 1950s, 0.77" x 0.88", $120–180.

Butterfly earrings, mosaic overlay, Thomasine Shack, no hallmark, 1950s, 0.81" x 0.84", $120–180.

Thomasine Shack made this butterfly pin in the mosaic overlay style in the 1950s. It is a very tiny piece, measuring only 0.83 inch tall. However, three stamped silver drops set in a triangular form are identical to those described above, and its upper wings are similar to those on her bigger piece. It also has strips of turquoise between the black and white parts of the upper wings. It consists of blue/green turquoise, orange spiny oyster, white mother of pearl, and black jet.

In the 1950s, Thomasine Shack made these butterfly earrings in the mosaic overlay style. They are identical in color combination to those pictured in the same book that features her butterfly bolo, on the same page, in the upper right corner (Bassman, 1992, p. 13). They measure 0.88 inch tall and consist of green turquoise, orange spiny oyster, white mother of pearl, and black jet.

The same artist made these butterfly earrings in the mosaic overlay style in the 1950s. They are identical to her smaller butterfly design, although they have a different color combination. They measure 0.84 inches tall and consist of green turquoise, orange spiny oyster, white mother of pearl, and black jet.

As I noted earlier, she made a butterfly necklace in a totally different design which can be found in *Zuni: The Art and the People*, Vol. 1 (Bell, 1975, pp. 34-35). In my opinion, her older butterfly designs are much better than the ones made in the 1970s. The same book features her Rainbow Man pieces in this alternate design, as well. I do not understand why these changes in her design were made.

Butterfly pin, channel inlay, Della Casi, no hallmark, 1940s–50s, 0.84" x 0.74", $80–120.

Butterfly ring, channel inlay, Frank Dishta, no hallmark, 1940s–50s, 0.66" x 0.72", $120–180.

Butterfly earrings, channel inlay, Della Casi, no hallmark, 1940s–50s, 0.80" x 0.68", $120–180.

Frank Dishta made this butterfly ring in the channel inlay style in the 1940s or 1950s. It measures 0.72 inch tall.

In the 1940s or 1950s, Della Casi made these inlay butterfly earrings in the channel inlay style. They measure 0.68 inch tall.

The same artist made this butterfly pin in the channel inlay style in the 1940s or 1950s. It was converted from an earring, probably because another one was lost. It measures 0.74 inch tall.

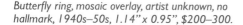

Butterfly ring, mosaic overlay, artist unknown, no hallmark, 1940s–50s, 1.14" x 0.95", $200–300.

Butterfly pin, mosaic overlay, Lee Edaakie, no hallmark, 1940s–50s, 1.41" x 1.20", $160–240.

Butterfly pin, channel inlay, Henry Owelicio, no hallmark, 1970s–80s, 1.22" x 1.48", $300–450. Courtesy of Thelma Sheche.

In the 1940s or 1950s, an unknown artist made this butterfly ring in the mosaic overlay style. Although it is very tiny, measuring 0.95 inch tall, it is colorful and well-made. It has four inlaid dots on both wings. It was attributed variously to Lee Edaakie, Betty Natachu, Harry Deutsawe, and Mary Kallestewa. Whoever made it, it is without doubt one of the best butterfly rings. Its upper and lower wings are heart-shaped.

Lee Edaakie made this butterfly pin in the mosaic inlay style in the 1940s or 1950s. It has two inlaid dots on each wing, and a complicated inlay pattern in the wings as well as in the body. It measures 1.20 inches tall and consists of blue/green turquoise, red abalone, white mother of pearl, and black jet.

In the 1970s or 1980s, Henry Owelicio made this butterfly pin in the channel inlay style. One day in November, 2011, I found Thelma Sheche wearing it on her blouse. I thought I had not seen a similar piece before and felt it was unique and very good. I asked Thelma whose work it was and she told me it was Henry Owelicio's. This pin was presented to her directly from him. This was the first time I heard his name. It measures 1.48 inches.

Butterfly pin, mosaic overlay, Harry Deutsawe, silver work by Leonard Martza, LM, lapidary work 1980s and silver work 2009, 1.94" x 1.82", $300–450.

Harry Deutsawe made this butterfly pin in the mosaic overlay style in the 1980s, and Leonard Martza set it on silver in 2009. When I got it, I did not know who did the lapidary work. However, when I asked Leonard Martza and Genevieve Tucson, who made my older Sin Face bolo with a lot of inlaid dots, Genevieve answered promptly that it was Harry's. She also showed me his lapidary works, pasted on cardboard, that were left to her. His pieces always have a silver platelet among stones and shell, even if made in the mosaic overlay style.

As for his butterfly design, there is always a heart-shaped pattern in the forewings and sometimes in the hind wings as well. His niece, Elvira Kiyite Leekity, makes a similar butterfly design, but, instead of a heart pattern, there are deformed heart shapes in both forewings. It measures 1.82 inches tall and consists of blue/green turquoise, red spiny oyster, white mother of pearl, black jet, and silver platelet.

Butterfly pin, mosaic overlay, Harry Deutsawe, no hallmark, 1950s–60s, 2.18" x 1.79", $300–450.

Butterfly pin, mosaic overlay, Harry Deutsawe, no hallmark, 1950s–60s, 1.62" x 1.45", $300–450.

Butterfly bolo, mosaic overlay, Winnie Wallace(?), no hallmark, 1940s–50s, 1.89" x 1.28", $300–450.

In the 1950s or 1960s, Harry Deutsawe made this butterfly pin in the mosaic overlay style. We can clearly see a heart-shaped pattern in the forewings and hind wings on the both sides. Below its body, we will also notice three stamped silver drops set in the reverse triangular form. It measures 1.79 inches tall and consists of blue turquoise, red spiny oyster, white mother of pearl, black jet, and silver platelet.

The same artist made this smaller butterfly pin in the mosaic overlay style in the 1950s or 1960s. Although it is smaller, it is almost identical to his butterfly pin just described at left. In addition, their silver works are almost identical as well, especially in their placement of silver drops. It measures 1.45 inches tall and consists of blue turquoise, red spiny oyster, white mother of pearl, black jet, and silver platelet.

Winnie Wallace probably made this butterfly bolo, done in the mosaic overlay style in the 1940s or 1950s. It has a handmade clasp with a single silver plate, which is folded like a tube, the center of which bolo strings can be pushed through. It measures 1.28 inches tall and consists of blue/green turquoise, orange spiny oyster, white clam shell, and black jet.

Butterfly pin, mosaic overlay, Winnie Wallace, no hallmark, 1970s–80s, 2.40" x 1.61", $300–450.

Butterfly pin, mosaic overlay, Winnie Wallace, no hallmark, 1960s–70s, 2.31" x 1.63", $300–450.

Butterfly bolo, mosaic overlay, Winnie Wallace, no hallmark, 1960s–80s, 2.30" x 1.75", $300–450.

In the 1960s or 1970s, Winnie Wallace made this butterfly bolo in the mosaic overlay style. It is more complicatedly crafted than the last one described on the last page. It measures 1.75 inches tall and consists of blue/green turquoise, orange spiny oyster, white clam shell, and black jet.

Winnie also made this butterfly pin in the mosaic overlay style in the 1970s or 1980s. It features the same stamp applied on the silver wire of Winnie's first bolo, described on the last page, and may have commercial silver drops. Therefore, its silver work was done by the same silversmith, after the previous bolo's. It measures 1.61 inches tall and consists of green turquoise, orange spiny oyster, white mother of pearl, and black jet.

This butterfly pin, made in the mosaic overlay style in the 1960s or 1970s, is also attributed to Winnie Wallace. It has a slightly complicated body pattern and uses flattened, twisted silver wire in place of the stamped silver wire in two of her other pins. It uses smaller commercial silver drops as well. It measures 1.63 inches tall and consists of blue turquoise, orange spiny oyster, white mother of pearl, and black jet.

Butterfly pin, mosaic overlay, Betty Natachu, Natachu, 1960s–70s, 1.27" x 1.18", $180–270.

Butterfly watch tips, mosaic overlay, Betty Natachu, G B, 2000s, 0.96" x 0.89", $200–300.

Butterfly bracelet, mosaic overlay, Juralita Lamy, no hallmark, 1950s–60s, central medallion 1.51" x 1.49", $400–600.

Betty Natachu made this butterfly pin in the mosaic overlay style, and one of her sons set it on silver after her husband passed on. When I showed this to her, she could not identify it as hers, but, her son, told her he had set it for her. It is a tiny piece, measuring only 1.18 inches tall. Considering this smaller size, her lapidary skill is amazing. She is truly a queen of miniature mosaic overlay artists. It consists of blue turquoise, red coral, white mother of pearl, and black jet.

The same artist made these watch tips in the mosaic overlay style in the 1980s. They have a hallmark, "G B Natachu." Her husband, Gillerimo Natachu, set her lapidary work on silver. Her minute lapidary skills amaze us still more, as the tips measure only 0.89 inches tall. They consist of deep blue turquoise, red coral, white mother of pearl, and black jet.

Juralita Lamy made this butterfly bracelet in the mosaic overlay style in the 1950s or 1960s. There is one center medallion surrounded by a smaller medallion on either side. Antennae of these butterflies are stamped with a crescent-shaped die. There is a similar butterfly set in *Turquoise Jewelry of the Indians of the Southwest*, although my piece looks older, and its silver work is more complicated than those in the set (Bennett 1973, p. 115). This set of bracelet, ring, and earrings cost $90 in 1972. My bracelet is adorned with five silver leaves in three different designs. The central butterfly measures 1.49 inches tall including antennae and consists of blue turquoise, white mother of pearl, and black jet.

Butterfly bracelet, mosaic overlay, Juralita Lamy, no hallmark, 1960s–70s, central medallion 1.40" x 1.55", $300–450.

Butterfly ring, mosaic overlay, Juralita Lamy, no hallmark, 1950s–60s, 1.10" x 1.01", $150–225.

Juralita also made this matching butterfly ring in the mosaic overlay style in the 1950s or 1960s. It is exactly the same as the smaller butterflies on the sides of the bracelet, including the stamped silver antennae. It measures 1.01 inches tall and consists of blue turquoise, white mother of pearl, and black jet.

In the 1960s or 1970s, Juralita Lamy made this butterfly bracelet in the mosaic overlay style. It is almost the same as the bracelet described above, except for the stamp on the antennae. Together, the bracelet and the following ring, pin, and earrings, constitute a set. The central butterfly measures 1.55 inches tall and consists of blue turquoise, white mother of pearl, and black jet. The inlaid turquoise dots enhance the attractiveness of this elegant butterfly bracelet.

Butterfly ring, mosaic overlay, Juralita Lamy, no hallmark, 1960s–70s, 0.97" x 1.00", $120–180.

The same artist made this butterfly ring in the mosaic overlay style in the 1960s or 1970s. It measures only 1.00 inch tall.

Butterfly pin, mosaic overlay, Juralita Lamy, no hallmark, 1960s–70s, 1.4" x 1.72", $150–225.

This is a butterfly pin made by Juralita Lamy in the mosaic overlay style in the 1960s or 1970s. It is almost same as the central butterfly of the bracelet in the set. It measures 1.72 inches tall, including silver drops under the lower wings.

Butterfly earrings, mosaic overlay, Juralita Lamy, no hallmark, 1960s–70s, 1.00" x 1.14", $150–225.

These matching earrings were made by Juralita Lamy in the mosaic overlay style in the 1960s or 1970s. They have snapped clasps. They measure 1.14 inches tall.

Butterfly pin, mosaic overlay, Juralita Lamy, no hallmark, 1950s–60s, 1.4" x 1.72", $180–270.

Juralita made this butterfly pin as well, in the mosaic overlay style, in the 1950s or 1960s. Its silver antennae are stamped using the same dies as her first set. It has no silver leaf between its antennae. It measures 1.72 inches tall and consists of blue/green turquoise and black jet.

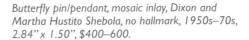

Butterfly pin/pendant, mosaic inlay, Dixon and Martha Hustito Shebola, no hallmark, 1950s–70s, 2.84" x 1.50", $400–600.

Butterfly pin, mosaic inlay, Mary Jane Boone, no hallmark, 1950s–70s, 2.37" x 2.17", $400–600.

Butterfly earrings, mosaic overlay, Juralita Lamy, no hallmark, 1960s–70s, 0.88" x 0.79", $150–225.

In the 1950s or 1960s, Juralita made these butterfly earrings in the mosaic overlay style. They had screw-in clasps on their backs when they were made, which were later converted into French hooks. It measures 0.79 inches tall.

Dixon and Martha Hustito Shebola made this butterfly pin in the mosaic inlay style sometime between the 1950s and 1970s. Inside its larger wings, we can see a much smaller wing-like pattern which is inlaid with white mother of pearl. To this white wing-like pattern, the artists add large outer wings. Each of the four channels houses turquoise and pink shell parts inside. These compartments are constructed with more complex lines than any other piece in this book. Due to this complexity, their lapidary skills are considered incredible. We can observe a trace of cement only in one position. This is true stone-to-stone inlay. It measures 1.50 inches tall.

Sometime between the 1950s and 1970s, Mary Jane Boone made this butterfly pin in the mosaic inlay style. Mary is a sister of Myra Tucson. This is a well-designed and well-executed butterfly pin. We can see almost no cement between silver wall and stone/shell. As silver compartments are made first and stones and shells are cut to fit to them later, it is rare to see no cement between silver and stone/shell. In addition, this butterfly design itself is beautiful. It measures 2.17 inches tall and consists of blue turquoise, orange spiny oyster, pinkish mother of pearl, and dark brown pen shell.

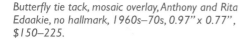

Butterfly tie tack, mosaic overlay, Anthony and Rita Edaakie, no hallmark, 1960s–70s, 0.97" x 0.77", $150–225.

Butterfly earrings, channel inlay, artist unknown, no hallmark, 1960s–70s, 0.62" x 0.30", $60–90.

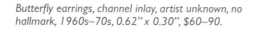

Butterfly bolo, mosaic overlay, Velma Lesansee, no hallmark, 1960s–80s, 2.33" x 2.38", $300–450.

Anthony and Rita Edaakie made this butterfly tie tack in the mosaic overlay style in the 1950s or 1970s. It measures only 0.77 inches tall, including its silver antennae. Considering this smaller size, it is extremely well-made. Using a thin strip of black jet, each wing is divided in half, and the outer parts of the upper wings are divided again into orange and white halves. It consists of green turquoise, orange spiny oyster, white mother of pearl, and black jet.

In the 1960s or 1970s, an unknown artist made these extremely tiny butterfly earrings in the mosaic inlay style. Although we cannot see it clearly, these minute turquoise pieces are cut, polished, and then set in these compartments. They might have been made by Ben Eustace or his family members. It measures 0.30 inches tall.

Velma Lesansee made this butterfly bolo in the mosaic overlay style sometime between the 1960s and 1980s. Ten black dots are inlaid in the wings, and two smaller black dots are inlaid in its eyes. It measures 2.38 inches tall and consists of iridescent abalone, gold lip mother of pearl, white mother of pearl, and black jet. Even without red or orange, it looks gorgeous.

Butterfly pin, mosaic inlay, Reyes Neha, no hallmark, 1960s, 1.34" x 1.39", $100–150.

Reyes Neha made this mosaic inlay butterfly pin in the 1960s. A similar butterfly set is attributed to Randolph Nahohai by Kennedy Museum of Art, Ohio University. However, my Zuni friend, Milford Nahohai, told me he did not think his older brother made this kind of butterfly jewelry in the mosaic inlay style. These kinds of butterfly designs are made by Anselm Wallace and Reyes Neha. As the butterfly design by Anselm Wallace is a little different at the uppermost part of the wings, we can deny the possibility of Wallace as its artist. In addition, an almost identical butterfly ring on our Historic Zuni Jewelry Facebook page is hallmarked "R. Neha" on its back. Consequently, I would like to attribute this pin to Reyes Neha. His butterfly necklace is featured in the book *Zuni Jewelry* (Bassman, 1992, p. 51). It measures 1.39 inches tall and consists of blue turquoise, white mother of pearl, and black jet.

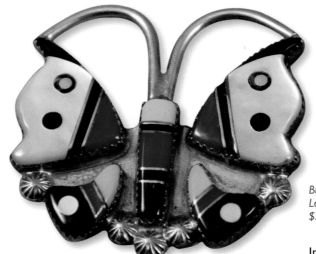

Butterfly pin, mosaic overlay, Elvira Kiyite
Leekity, D & E Leekity, 1990, 1.79" x 1.76",
$200–300.

Butterfly pin/pendant, mosaic inlay, Reyes Neha, R. N., 1970s, 0.94" x 0.93", $80–120.

The same artist made this butterfly pin/pendant in the mosaic inlay style in the 1970s. It is stamped "R. N. Sterling" on its back. It measures 0.93 inches tall and consists of green turquoise, red coral, white mother of pearl, and black jet.

In the 1990s, Elvira Leekity made this mosaic overlay butterfly pin. It is very similar to the one made by her uncle, Harry Deutsawe. However, her piece is different from his in that, unlike Deutsawe's butterfly pins, there is no clear heart shape in the forewing. Besides this point, it is very difficult to differentiate their pieces. It measures 1.76 inches tall and consists of blue turquoise, red coral, white mother of pearl, black jet, and silver.

As Bedinger notes, Zuni artists are always unique and individualistic when they create their own design in a motif such as a butterfly. This was also true when they created their own designs in their own cultural motifs such as Knifewing and Rainbow Man. According to Bedinger (1973, p. 202):

> Zunis tend to cling to conventional designs. They do not reproduce pictographs, as the Navajos do with humor and charm. Mimbres and Hohokam figures are ignored also, although these fascinating creatures are well adapted to the mosaic technique. Yet the tribe does not lack originality. Butterflies, ever popular, are elaborate and varied.

We cannot help but be amazed by individual Zuni artists who have created various and unique designs of butterfly, which they have similarly accomplished with various designs of Knifewing, Rainbow Man, Sun Face, Hopi Bird, several Kachinas, and Ceremonial Dancers.

2 Dragonfly

Dragonfly is a motif which is closely associated with water and is extremely important to Zuni people and culture. It is frequently depicted on Zuni pots and sacred cornmeal bowls in Zuni pottery (Nahohai and Phelps, 1995, p. 32, 44). As cornmeal is used as an offering to Kachinas who bring rain on the Zuni land, it is natural that the sacred cornmeal bowl is accompanied with dragonflies, as well as turquoise. Frank (1990) comments on the double-barred cross design:

> It is hard to say whether the naja seen here (and in general) is a version of a Christian cross or modified dragonfly in the Plains and Pueblo Indian Cultures. On the jar above the dragonfly is a butterfly; both figures are symbols for water, especially at Zuni. (p.158)

Although I am not certain whether butterfly is a symbol for water in Zuni or not, dragonfly—along with Frog, tadpole, and tortoise (McManis, 1995, p. 21)—is surely such a symbol and very important for the Zunis and their culture.

In the Adair book, two dragonfly pins carved by Teddy Weahkee and set on silver by Okweene Neese are included (Adair, 1944, p.149, 192, plate 23D).

The C. G. Wallace Auction Catalogue includes only six pieces, compared with twenty-five in the Butterfly design. Out of these six dragonflies, five are made by John Leekity (Gordon Leak), and the other is made by Juan de Dios. It seems strange that only two artists made jewelry in this design. It might be because dragonfly jewelry had not appealed to the traders and their clients back in those years. However, in my collection, I have more than ten dragonfly pieces made by various Zuni artists.

In the 1940s or 1950s, Leekya Deyuse made this dragonfly pin in the mosaic inlay in jet style, which was set by his son-in-law, Frank Vacit. It was confirmed as their joint work by one of Frank's daughters. It is similar to the ones usually attributed to John Leekity. However, as she attributed my Knifewing pieces to Dexter Cellicion, which had formerly been attributed to Leekya or John Leekity, I believe this attribution is probably correct. There are two inlaid turquoise dots for its eyes and an additional six alongside its lower body. These six dots may symbolize the rain. It is very difficult to inlay these dots in the jet background because jet is a very hard material and lacks flexibility, unlike shells. It measures 1.56 inches tall and consists of blue turquoise, red spiny oyster, white mother of pearl, and the black jet background.

Walter Nakatewa made this dragonfly bolo in the raised mosaic inlay in a spiny oyster shell style in the 1940s or 1950s. It has W-shaped silver platelet clasps, as well as a pendant bail on the back. This shell inlay is the traditional method in which Zunis have made their adornments for more than a thousand years. However, Nakatewa set the inlaid shell on silver instead of putting holes into the shell for the pendant. I love very much that this is reminiscent of one thousand years of tradition. The dragonfly looks primitive but attractive. Its turquoise and jet inlay in the upper one third of the spiny oyster shell is eye-pleasing as well. It measures 2.80 inches tall and consists of blue/green turquoise, black jet, and orange spiny oyster.

Dragonfly pin, mosaic overlay, Leo Poblano, no hallmark, 1940s–50s, 2.02" x 1.06", $1000–1500.

Dragonfly bracelet, mosaic overlay, Ida Vacit Poblano, no hallmark, 1940s–60s, 2.26" x 1.39", $1200–1800.

Leo Poblano made this dragonfly pin in the mosaic overlay style in the 1940s or 1950s. As it has narrow wings, I classify it as a dragonfly. Although it is a tiny piece, measuring only 1.06 inches tall, it is a very attractive piece of jewelry. It consists of blue/green turquoise, orange spiny oyster, and black jet.

Ida Vacit Poblano made this dragonfly bracelet in the mosaic overlay style sometime between the 1940s and 1960s. Although it is made in the mosaic overlay style, its antennae are inlaid in the black jet background, and small green turquoise dots are added above its antennae. It measures 1.39 inches tall with the medallion and consists of blue/green turquoise, orange spiny oyster, white clam shell, and black jet.

Dragonfly pin/pendant converted from bolo, mosaic inlay in jet, Ida Vacit Poblano, no hallmark, 1940s–50s, 2.79" x 2.48", $1000–1500.

Sometime between the 1940s and 1960s, Ida Vacit Poblano made this dragonfly pin/pendant in the mosaic inlay in jet style. It seems to be converted from bolo, because there is only one W-shaped bolo clasp on its back. When I showed this to my friend, Milford Nahohai, he moved his fingers back and forth on it, closing his eyes. I asked him what he was doing. He replied that he appreciated how smoothly his fingers could move on its surface, as if the whole of it were made of one material. Although I can see some lines on the background and the entirety is made of several parts, I can feel no gap among the parts. It is perfectly done. In addition, the Dragonfly itself is well-designed and well-executed. It measures 2.48 inches tall and consists of green turquoise, red coral, white mother of pearl, and black jet.

Dragonfly pins, channel inlay, Henry Owelicio, no hallmark, 2000s, 1.37" x 1.21", $200–300. Courtesy of Lorandina Sheche.

Henry Owelicio made these dragonfly pins in the channel inlay style in the late 2000s. As I related earlier, in his biography, Henry gave these to Ilka Sheche's two daughters as birthday presents. They are 1.21 inches tall.

Dragonfly pin, channel inlay, Henry Owelicio, no hallmark, 1980s–90s, 0.94" x 1.04", $120–180.

Dragonfly pin, mosaic overlay, artist unknown, no hallmark, 1940s–60s, 1.87" x 2.55", $300–450.

Dragonfly pin/pendant, mosaic overlay, Bowman Paywa(?), no hallmark, 1940s–50s, 2.03" x 1.59", $300–450.

The same artist made this dragonfly pin in the channel inlay style in the 1980s or 1990s. Soon after I came to know his name and his designs of butterfly and dragonfly, I found this pin and got it in an online auction. It was the moment when my small dream came true. It measures only 1.04 inches tall.

An unknown artist made this dragonfly pin in the mosaic overlay style in the 1940s or 1960s. Its head, lower body, and wings are made with black jet, and each part of them is lowered where turquoise parts or white and orange parts are pasted. As for the antennae, both tips are lowered, but these places are set with no parts. This is a very unique method of the mosaic overlay style. Its silver base is stamped elaborately. It measures 2.55 inches tall and consists of green turquoise, orange spiny oyster, white clam shell, and black jet.

Bowman Paywa probably made this dragonfly pin/pendant, done in the mosaic overlay style in the 1940s or 1950s, although I am not very sure about this attribution. Its silver backing is stamped all around the dragonfly figure except for its antennae. Both tips of the base just above the body are cut and curled, and two silver drops are added onto them. This method seems very unique to me. It measures 1.59 inches tall and consists of blue/green turquoise, orange spiny oyster, white clam shell, and black jet.

Dragonfly bracelet, mosaic overlay, artist unknown, no hallmark, 1940s–1950s, 0.85" x 0.92", $200–300.

Dragonfly pin/pendant, cluster work, Leonard Martza, LM, 2008, 3.33" x 2.90", $300–450.

In the 1940s or 1950s, an unknown artist made this dragonfly bracelet in the mosaic overlay style. On both sides of the dragonfly, two cloud symbols are placed. These three figures all symbolize water and rain. This is the first example I have seen in this combination. It might have been made earlier than the estimated year of make. The dragonfly measures only 0.92 inches tall and consists of green turquoise and black jet.

Leonard Martza made this dragonfly pin/pendant, in the nugget work style in 2008. Stamped silver strips, silver wire, and silver drops are welded on the silver backing, and then, six legs are bent as they would look naturally. Lastly, various nuggets of stones such as blue and green turquoise and orange and red coral are set. This is rarely seen in Zuni jewelry. It measures 2.90 inches tall.

I have examined eleven samples of dragonfly pieces. As with the butterfly designs, we can also see a wide variety of dragonfly designs. Although I have not even attempted to collect more pieces than those featured in the C. G. Wallace Auction Catalogue, my collection still represents a wide variety.

Frog, Tortoise, and Bee

Frog and Tortoise are both associated with water and rain; therefore, they are important animals for Zunis. McManis notes:

Considered one of, if not the major Rain-bringing fetish, the frog is also associated with abundance and fertility.....Tortoises also have a rain association in addition to serving as a link to the Zuni ancestors. Frog and tortoise fetishes are some of the most frequently carved at Zuni. (1995, p. 24)

While various carvers have carved frog and tortoise in Zuni fetishes in large quantities, only a handful of jewelers/lapidaries have created frog and tortoise in Zuni jewelry. In the C. G. Wallace Collection Catalogue, we can find five frogs. Two out of the five were made by Leekya Deyuse and Teddy Weahkee, and one was made by Walter Nakatewa. The catalogue includes eight tortoises, and three were made by Leekya, Harold Tucson, and Della Casi. I have seen several frogs and a few tortoises in vintage Zuni jewelry over the last ten years.

I have collected only three frogs and two tortoises.

Frog pin/pendant, mosaic inlay, Leo Poblano, no hallmark, 1940s–50s, 2.21" x 1.49", $2000–3000.

Leo Poblano made this frog pin/pendant in the raised mosaic inlay style in the 1940s or 1950s. I found and got it at an antique Native American jewelry shop on the Santa Fe Plaza around ten years ago. Although it looks like it was made in the overlay style, raised, large black mother of pearl shell parts are set in the lowered silver channels. A silver wall around its eye is set higher than the frog body, and a round, white mother of pearl part is set in it. Twelve round turquoise dots are inlaid all around its body. This dot inlay greatly enhances the attractiveness of this frog. It measures 1.49 inches tall.

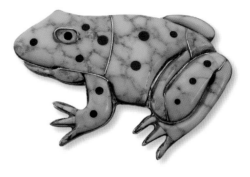

Frog pin/pendant, mosaic inlay, Leo Poblano, no hallmark, 2.18" x 1.53", 1950s, $1600–2400.

Leo also made this mosaic inlay frog pin/pendant in the 1950s. It was made using almost exactly the same method applied to the frog just described at left, except that some parts of the silver wall are set at the same level as the frog body. It measures 1.53 inches tall and consists of blue/green turquoise, white mother of pearl, and black jet. These two frogs are well-designed and well-executed.

Frog pin/pendant, mosaic inlay, Porfilio and Ann Sheyka, no hallmark, 1960s–70s, 1.87" x 1.95", $300–450.

Porfilio and Ann Sheyka made this frog pin/pendant in the mosaic inlay style in the 1960s or 1970s. While the last two frogs, made by Leo Poblano, are depicted from the standpoint of a 45-degree angle from the right, this frog is designed from directly above. Except for its front right arm, fifteen turquoise dots are inlaid all over its body, legs, and left arm, and two mother of pearl dots are inlaid in the right arm. Two black jet dots are inlaid in the white mother of pearl eyes, which are inlaid in the frog face. It measures 1.95 inches tall.

Turtle bolo, mosaic inlay, Rosemary and Dexter Cellicion, no hallmark, 1940s–50s, 1.37" x 1.70", $400–600.

Rosemary and Dexter Cellicion made this tortoise bolo in the mosaic inlay style in the 1940s or 1950s. It is designed from the standpoint of being directly above. Though it looks flat and static, it is cute. It measures 1.70 inches tall and consists of blue turquoise, orange spiny oyster, white mother of pearl, and black jet.

Turtle bolo, mosaic inlay, Rosemary and Dexter Cellicion, no hallmark, 1940s–50s, 1.42" x 1.76", $400–600.

The same couple made this tortoise bolo in the mosaic inlay style in the 1940s or 1950s. It is almost identical to their bolo just described, above, although the parts of its head consist of three instead of two sections, and the color combinations of the two are totally different. It measures 1.76 inches tall and consists of blue turquoise, red coral, white mother of pearl, and black jet.

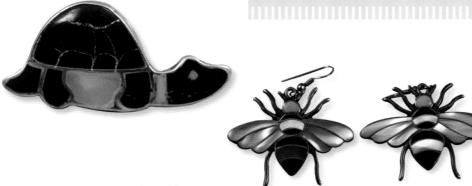

The last motif in this section is bee. This is the only such piece I have seen in vintage Zuni jewelry; in the C. G. Wallace Collection Auction Catalogue, insects are mentioned but no bee is included.

Turtle Tie tack, mosaic inlay, Dorothy and Bruce Zunie, no hallmark, 1950s–70s, 1.18" x 0.58", $160–240.

Bumble bee earrings, mosaic inlay, Leo Poblano(?), no hallmark, 1950s, 1.80" x 1.40", $300–450.

Dorothy and Bruce Zunie made this tortoise tie tack in the mosaic inlay style sometime between the 1950s and 1970s. We can see similar pieces even today, but they do not have the natural curves seen in this piece. It is very tiny (only 0.58 inches tall). Still, it is well-designed and well-made and looks very cute. It consists of blue turquoise, brown tortoise shell, and white mother of pearl.

Leo Poblano probably made these bumble bee earrings, done in the mosaic inlay style in the 1950s. They are extremely well-designed and well-executed. It's also possible that they might have been made by his daughter-in-law, Shirley Benn. They measure 1.40 inches tall and consist of blue turquoise, white mother of pearl, and black jet.

In summary, we have examined six pieces of jewelry in this section. Although there are not many pieces available, all are well-designed and well-executed. These rare pieces surely exhibit the outstanding talent of Zuni artists.

Birds

The *C. G. Wallace Auction Catalogue* features twenty-four Bird pieces (11.1 %) out of 217 samples. As for the kinds of birds, duck, owl, roadrunner, and peacock are mentioned; Leekya Deyuse, Walter Nahktewa, Theodore Edaakie, Annie Quam Gasper, Mary Kallestewa, Dan Simplicio, and Leo Poblano are listed as their creators. As for the time of their creation, only two pieces are specified, and both of them were made in the 1930s. As for the birds in general, according to McManis (1995, p.25), "Most birds are believed to carry prayers to the cloud and the sky, asking for rain and blessing".

Here, we classify birds into duck, eagle, roadrunner, owl, quail, phoenix, and others.

1 Ducks

These duck-in-flight pieces are absolutely marvelous, and I feel very sorry that in recent years, they have rarely been made.

Leo Poblano's ducks-in-flight pin is not in this voume, but it can be found in various other books (Ostler, et al, 1996. p. 101; Arizona Highways, August 1974. p. 45). It was made in the mosaic inlay style in 1951.

Wild duck bolo, mosaic inlay, Homer and Myra Vacit, no hallmark, 1940s–1950s, 2.45"x2.15", $1200–1800.

Homer and Myra Vacit made this duck-in-flight bolo in the mosaic inlay style in the 1940s or 1950s. They depict the moment when the duck swings its wings at the down-most position. It measures 2.15 inches tall and consists of green and blue turquoise, red coral, orange clam shell, iridescent abalone, white mother of pearl, and black jet.

Wild duck bolo, mosaic inlay, Lambert Homer Sr., no hallmark, 1940s–50s, 2.29" x 1.87", $1600–2400.

In the 1940s or 1950s, Lambert Homer Sr. made this duck-in-flight bolo in the mosaic inlay style. Its wings are set at the upper-most position and are about to move downward. The lower half of the wings is inlaid with turquoise in the channel inlay style. This application of style is often seen in Eagle pieces in Zuni jewelry. In addition, its upper halves of the wings are set with black-and-white parts. This color combination in black, white, and blue in its wings makes this duck beautiful and unique. It measures 1.87 inches tall and consists of blue green turquoise, orange spiny oyster, spotted cowrie shell, white mother of pearl, and black jet.

Wild duck bolo, mosaic inlay, Lambert Homer Sr.(?), no hallmark, 1940s–50s, 2.93" x 2.22", $1000–1500.

Lambert Homer Sr. probably made this duck-in-flight bolo, done in the mosaic inlay style in the 1940s or 1950s, although one of my informants attributes it to Elliot Qualo. The duck is flying just over the surface of a lake, which can be determined by the waves under the duck. The silver walls show a lot of curvature, which make cutting stone and shell parts extremely difficult. In addition, silver work, including file and stamp work, enhances the attractiveness of this pin. It measures 2.22 inches tall and consists of blue turquoise, orange spiny oyster, iridescent abalone, white mother of pearl, and black jet.

Wild duck bolo, mosaic overlay, artist unknown, no hallmark, 1940s–50s, 2.05" x 1.67", $300–450.

Wild duck bolo, mosaic inlay in clam shell, Elliot Qualo, no hallmark, 1940s–50s, 2.05" x 1.67", $1200–1800.

Wild duck pin/pendant, mosaic inlay, Howard Esalio(?), H. Esalio, 1970s–80s, 1.59" x 1.22", $100–150.

Judging by its double W-shaped bolo clasps, an unknown artist made this duck-in-flight bolo in the mosaic inlay style, in the 1940s or 1950s. One of my informants attributes it to Theodore Edaakie. It has turquoise nuggets for bolo tips. It measures 1.67 inches tall and consists of green turquoise, orange spiny oyster, dark brown pen shell, and white clam shell.

Elliot Qualo made this duck-in-flight bolo in the mosaic inlay in clam shell style in the 1940s or 1950s. Although there is no hallmark of his double antler on its back, its forms of bezel and stamped medallion edge clearly show it is his work. The bolo clasp consists of one W-shaped and one U-shaped silver platelet. There are intricate etchings on the wings which set high over its body and are about to move downward. It measures 1.67 inches tall and consists of blue/green turquoise, dark brown pen shell, light green serpentine, and white mother of pearl.

Based on the hallmark written with electric pencil, it's likely that Howard Esalio is the artist responsible for this duck-in-flight pin/pendant, made in the mosaic inlay style in the 1970s. It is not a masterpiece but a cute and lovely item. It measures 1.22 inches tall and consists of blue turquoise, iridescent abalone, spotted cowrie shell, orange abalone, white mother of pearl, and black jet.

The eagle is a sacred bird for the Zunis as well as for the Pueblo people. It mediates humans on the ground and the sacred beings in the sky, where they reside. At one Hopi pueblo, I saw an eagle being nurtured on the rooftop in order to be sacrificed for religious purposes. This species of eagle is designated as an endangered one, but is allowed to be raised and sacrificed only for native religious ceremony. Eagle feathers used to be used for outfits for religious dancers as well.

As for Zuni fetishes, an eagle is important as a protector of the upper region as well as a hunting fetish for rabbits or other small game (McManis, 1995, p. 17).

In Zuni, there are two eagle clans: the Golden Eagle Clan and the Bald Eagle Clan. However, the Bald Eagle seems to have been made much more in jewelry than the golden eagle, probably because of the outside demand for the former.

Eagle bolo, mosaic inlay, Della Casi(?), no hallmark, 1950s–60s, 2.28" x 2.57", $1200–1800.

Della Casi is probably responsible for this bald eagle bolo, made in the mosaic inlay style in the 1950s or 1960s. It catches a snake in its claws and is about to fly. This is a typical eagle design made frequently by various Zuni artists. Its wings are inlaid with turquoise in a kind of random pattern, which is typically used by Bernard Homer Sr.'s wife, Alice Leekya Homer. It measures 2.57 inches tall and consists of blue/green turquoise, spotted cowrie shell, white mother of pearl, and dark brown tortoise shell.

Eagle bolo, mosaic inlay, Della Casi, no hallmark, 1950s–60s, 2.54" x 3.07", $1200–1800.

The same artist made this bald eagle bolo in the mosaic inlay style in the 1950s or 1960s. Because it is bigger than the bolo just described, above, more feathers are present, and the eyes are different. In addition, the random patterns of turquoise channel inlay are a little different between the two. Except for these differences, these two pieces bear resemblance to each other, especially in the posture of eagles and the forms of the inlaid snakes. It measures 3.07 inches tall and consists of blue/green turquoise, spotted cowrie shell, dark brown turtle shell, and white mother of pearl.

Eagle bolo, mosaic inlay, John Lucio, no hallmark, 1950s–60s, 2.06" x 1.98", $300–400.

Eagle bolo, mosaic inlay, John Lucio, no hallmark, 1940s–50s, 2.19" x 2.18", $1000–1500.

Eagle pin converted from bolo, mosaic inlay, John and Cecilia Lucio, no hallmark, 1940s–50s, 2.37" x 1.66", $600–900.

John Lucio made this bald eagle bolo in the mosaic inlay style in the 1950s or 1960s. This bolo has two smaller but identical eagles for tips. These three eagles catch one snake each in their claws, although these snakes do not look realistic. The eagles have inlaid turquoise parts in the random pattern. It measures 1.98 inches tall and consists of blue/green turquoise, white mother of pearl, orange spiny oyster, and dark brown tortoise shell.

In the 1940s or 1950s, John Lucio made this bald eagle bolo in the mosaic inlay style. Its bolo clasp is made with two round silver wires on top and one U-shaped silver wire under them. The turquoise parts in its wings are not in the random pattern, but a simple geometric one. Two smaller eaglets are set for tips, which are almost identical to the tips on the bolo just described, above. It measures 2.18 inches tall and consists of blue turquoise, white mother of pearl, and dark brown tortoise shell.

John Lucio and his wife, Cecilia, made this bald eagle pin in the mosaic inlay style in the 1940s or 1950s. As there are four remaining welding marks, this piece had been made as a bolo and was converted to a pin. The two triangular pieces and one rectangular in its mouth and foot might be a snake the eagle may be eating on the ground. It measures 1.66 inches tall and consists of blue turquoise, orange spiny oyster, iridescent abalone, white mother of pearl and black jet.

*Eagle bolo, mosaic inlay,
artist unknown,
no hallmark,
1940s–50s,
1.99" x 2.56",
$1000–1500.*

*Eagle bolo, mosaic inlay,
Edward Beyuka,
no hallmark,
mid–1950s,
1.99" x 2.56",
$1000–1500.*

*Eagle pendant, carving, Sarah Neese, no hallmark,
1950s–60s, 1.04" x 1.13", $200–300.*

In the 1940s or 1950s, an unknown artist made this bald eagle bolo in the mosaic inlay style. It has two W-shaped silver wires as a clasp. One informant attributed this to Elliot Qualo or Juan Qualo Jr. The etchings on its neck, back, and tails are rare for early Zuni pieces. The eagle has a silver snake in its mouth. It measures 2.56 inches tall and consists of blue/green turquoise, white mother of pearl, and black jet.

Edward Beyuka made this bald eagle bolo in the mosaic inlay style in the mid-1950s. It has a silver snake in its mouth, extends its wings wide, and appears to be flying. The bolo slide has two matching eagle feet as tips. It measures 2.56 inches tall and consists of blue turquoise, iridescent abalone, white mother of pearl, and dark brown tortoise shell.

It's probable that Sarah Neese is responsible for this turquoise eagle pendant, made in the carving style sometime between the 1940s and 1960s. It looks like a chimaera of Knifewing and eagle to me. However, one of my informants insisted it was an eagle. There are carvings on the wings and tail which signify feathers. These remind me of all the turquoise Knifewing carvings made by Leekya Deyuse. There is a small dimple on its head which represents an eye. It measures 1.13 inches tall.

*Eagle bolo, mosaic inlay,
Virgil and Shirley Benn,
Virgil and Shirley Benn,
1972, eagle 4.57" x 3.76",
rabbit 1.63" x 0.96,
$800–1200.*

*Eagle bolo, silver overlay/mosaic inlay, Jake Livingston,
J-l. Livingston, 1960s–80s, 2.14" x 2.77", $1000–
1500.*

*Eagle bolo, mosaic inlay, Gary and Paulinis Vacit, no
hallmark, 1940s–50s, 1.87" x 1.61", $300–450.*

Gary and Paulinis Vacit made this bald eagle bolo in the mosaic inlay style in the 1940s or 1950s. It looks like a Hopi Bird, but its head suggests it is an eagle. It measures 1.61 inches tall and consists of blue/green turquoise, red coral, white mother of pearl, and black jet.

Virgil and Shirley Benn made this bald eagle bolo in the raised and etched mosaic inlay style in 1972. The eagle is about to catch a rabbit. It is a very rare design. The eagle extends its wings wide and has the look of a real hunter. The cute rabbit is trying to escape from the dangerous claws of the eagle. This is really a one-of-a-kind piece. The eagle and rabbit measure 3.76 inches and 0.96 inches tall, respectively, and consist of dark brown tortoise shell, red coral, orange abalone, and white mother of pearl.

Sometime between the 1960s and 1980s, Jake Livingston made this bald eagle bolo in the silver overlay and mosaic inlay styles. Although this eagle design may not look unique to this artist, the execution of the raised and etched mosaic inlay exceeds far beyond average. It shows his technical excellence and predicts his success as a true creative artist in the future. It measures 2.77 inches tall and consists of blue/green turquoise, red coral, orange spiny oyster, iridescent abalone, white mother of pearl, and dark brown tortoise shell.

3 Roadrunner

Roadrunners have been made in large quantities by various Zuni artists. However, the famous C. G. Wallace Auction Catalogue features only three roadrunner pieces: two roadrunner pins by Theodore Edaakie and one tie tack by an unknown artist. As roadrunner fetishes have rarely been carved, a roadrunner design might not be native to Zuni culture. It may be a newly conceived one for tourists, based on the cartoon characters coyote and roadrunner.

Roadrunner bolo, mosaic inlay, Merle Edaakie, no hallmark, 1940s–50s, 2.54" x 1.93", $1200–1800.

Merle Edaakie made this roadrunner bolo in the mosaic inlay style in the 1940s or 1950s. The unique characteristics of this roadrunner design reside in the complex composition of its tail and its round face. The tail composition reminds me of the roadrunner pin from the book, *Turquoise Jewelry* (Schiffer, 1990, p.19), even though the composition of the one from Schiffer's book is simpler. The partly raised and carved mosaic inlay style reminds me of the technique frequently used by Edward Beyuka. It measures 1.93 inches tall and consists of blue turquoise, red coral, spotted cowrie shell, iridescent abalone, white mother of pearl, and dark brown tortoise shell.

Roadrunner pin, mosaic inlay, Merle Edaakie, no hallmark, 1950s–60s, 2.03" x 1.19", $200–300.

The same artist made this roadrunner pin, in the mosaic inlay style in the 1950s or 1960s. It is almost identical to the roadrunner pin in Shiffer's book mentioned at left. The only difference is their faces—the latter has a white part around its eye. The design of Merle's pin reminds me of the one made by Charlotte Dishta. However, her roadrunner pieces are usually smaller and use red coral in their bodies. It measures 1.19 inches tall and consists of iridescent abalone, white mother of pearl, spotted cowrie shell, and brown tortoise shell.

Roadrunner pin, mosaic inlay, artist unknown, no hallmark, 1940s–50s, 2.73" x 2.06", $300–450.

Roadrunner pin, mosaic inlay, Edward Beyuka, no hallmark, 1950s–60s, 2.80" x 1.74", $200–300.

Roadrunner bolo, mosaic inlay, Edward Beyuka, EAB, 1950s–60s, 2.84" x 1.76", $500–750.

In the 1940s or 1950s, an unknown artist made this roadrunner pin/pendant in the mosaic inlay style. One of my informants named as a possible artist Paul Leekity, a son of Nora Leekity. It looks very classical. There is a yucca flower in the background, and its leaves are depicted with silver wires. Stamped silver drops may be rocks. It measures 2.06 inches tall and consists of blue turquoise, red coral, iridescent abalone, white mother of pearl, and black jet.

Edward Beyuka made this roadrunner pin in the mosaic inlay style in the 1950s or 1960s. Even though his hallmark is not present, its use of wide silver wall certifies this attribution. However, it is also attributed to Homer Vacit by one of my informants. The inlay is all flash except for the raised and carved inlay in its crest. It measures 1.74 inches tall and consists of blue/green turquoise, spotted cowrie shell, tortoise shell, white mother of pearl, black jet, and unidentified colorful stone.

In the 1950s or 1960s the same artist made this roadrunner bolo in the mosaic inlay style. This bolo has his hallmark of "EAB" on its back. Its use of wide silver walls is similar to the pin just described, above. Its complex inlay pattern on its tail is similar to the ones made by Merle Edaakie. It measures 1.76 inches tall and consists of blue/green turquoise, red coral, spotted cowrie shell, iridescent abalone, white mother of pearl, and black jet.

Roadrunner bolo, mosaic inlay, Edward Beyuka, no hallmark, 1950s–60s, 1.95" x 1.36", $200–300.

Roadrunner bolo, mosaic inlay, Blake and Velma Lesansee, no hallmark, 1980s, 2.60" x 1.38", $400–600.

Roadrunner bolo, mosaic inlay, Blake and Velma Lesansee, no hallmark, 1960s–70s, 2.55" x 1.47", $400–600.

Edward also made this smaller roadrunner bolo in the mosaic inlay style in the 1980s. Although it does not have his hallmark, its use of wide silver wall reminds me of Edward Beyuka's work. However, one of my informants attributed it to Lambert Homer Jr. It measures 1.36 inches tall and consists of blue/green turquoise, spotted cowrie shell, and dark brown turtle shell.

Velma and Blake Lesansee made this roadrunner bolo in the mosaic inlay style in the 1980s. The half-circular stamp work on the bottom is a kind of signature of their work. It measures 1.38 inches tall and consists of blue turquoise, red coral, purple lip mother of pearl, white mother of pearl, and dark brown pen shell.

Again, in the 1980s, Velma and Blake made this roadrunner bolo in the mosaic inlay style. We can notice the same half-circular stamps on the bottom. It measures 1.47 inches tall and consists of blue/green turquoise, red coral, white mother of pearl, and dark brown pen shell.

Roadrunner bracelet, mosaic inlay, Theodore and Margaret Edaakie, no hallmark, 1960s–1970s, central figure 2.46" x 1.62", $800–1200.

Roadrunner pin, mosaic inlay, Theodore and Margaret Edaakie, no hallmark, 1960s–70s, 3.74" x 2.12", $400–600.

Opposite: Roadrunner bolo, mosaic inlay, Theodore and Margaret Edaakie, no hallmark, 1960s–70s, 2.32" x 1.03", $400–600.

Theodore and Margaret Edaakie made this Roadrunner pin in the mosaic inlay style in the 1960s or 1970s. It is not made in a flush inlay, but a slightly raised inlay in which each stone is individually polished perfectly and set in the channels. Its body is made in the random pattern as Alice Leekya Homer usually does. The stamp work along the upper side and stamped silver drop on its head are unique to them. It measures 2.12 inches tall and consists of blue turquoise, red coral, iridescent abalone, orange clam shell, white mother of pearl, and black jet.

Theodore and Margaret also made this roadrunner bracelet in the mosaic inlay style in the 1960s or 1970s. The roadrunner design is identical to the one just described, above, except for the use of a long triangular eye instead of the round eye in the pin. The stamp work along its upper side and stamped silver drops over its head and neck are also identical. The three consecutive half-circular stamps on the silver wires on the bracelet may be unique to Theodore and Margaret's silver work. The roadrunner measures 1.62 inches tall and consists of blue turquoise, red coral, gold lip mother of pearl, white mother of pearl, black jet, and grey stone or shell.

The same couple also made this roadrunner bolo with matching tips in the mosaic inlay style in the 1950s or 1960s. This bolo has silver leaves and three stamped silver drops under the roadrunner's legs. In addition to these silver works, the stamped silver platelets above the bird's neck, back, tail and under the legs are identical with the two pieces just described, above. Its lapidary work is similar to the following bolo. It measures 1.50 inches tall and consists of green turquoise, red coral, spotted cowrie shell, white mother of pearl, and black jet.

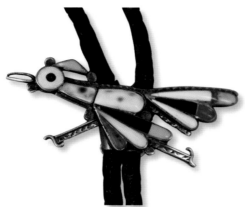

Roadrunner bolo, mosaic inlay, Theodore and Margaret Edaakie, no hallmark, 1950s–60s, 2.86" x 1.59", $400–600.

Also in the 1950s or 1960s, Theodore and Margaret made this roadrunner bolo in the mosaic inlay style. Its silver work along its upper side and stamped silver drops are identical to their pin and bracelet described above, although there is no random pattern inlay in its body. It measures 1.59 inches tall and consists of blue turquoise, red coral, spotted cowrie shell, white mother of pearl, and black jet.

Roadrunner bolo, mosaic inlay, Theodore and Margaret Edaakie, no hallmark, 1950s–60s, 2.28" x 1.18", $400–600.

This roadrunner bolo is also attributed to Theodore and Margaret Edaakie, and was made in the mosaic inlay style in the 1950s or 1960s. Although it is smaller, it is almost identical to their roadrunner bolos just described, above, including its silver work. It measures 1.18 inches tall and consists of blue turquoise, red coral, spotted cowrie shell, white mother of pearl, and black jet.

Roadrunner tie tack, mosaic inlay, artist unknown, no hallmark, 1960s–70s, 2.61" x 1.38", $200–300.

An unknown artist made this roadrunner tie tack in the mosaic inlay style in the 1960s or 1970s. One of my informants attributed it to Gary and Paulinis Vacit or Theodore and Margaret Edaakie. I am not sure about these attributions. The unique feature of this roadrunner design is that its head and crest are created as one piece. It measures 1.38 inches tall and consists of blue/green turquoise, red coral, spotted cowrie shell, iridescent abalone, and dark brown tortoise shell.

Roadrunner bolo, mosaic inlay, artist unknown, no hallmark, 1940s–50s, 2.37" x 1.05", $200–300.

This is a roadrunner bolo made by an unknown artist in the mosaic inlay style and, based on the W-shaped and U-shaped hand-made wire clasps, probably completed in the 1940s or 1950s. Although one of my informants attributed it to Theodore Edaakie, I am not certain about this attribution because it is too different from his well-known roadrunner design. Since the design of this roadrunner bolo is almost identical to the one signed by Fred Weekoty, it might have been made by some member of the Weekoty family. While the roadrunner itself is made in the mosaic inlay style, two plants or rocks on the ground are set, using bezels. The bow-shaped silver stamps are identical to the following roadrunner pin, made by the same artist. The stamps on its legs are similar to Theodore Edaakie's roadrunner bolo described earlier. It measures 1.05 inches tall and consists of green turquoise, orange spiny oyster, iridescent abalone, white mother of pearl, and black jet.

Roadrunner pin, mosaic inlay, artist unknown, no hallmark, 1940s–50s, 2.59" x 1.06", $200–300.

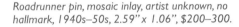

The same unknown artist made this roadrunner pin in the mosaic inlay style in the 1940s or 1950s. While the roadrunner bolo has a round eye inlaid directly in its face, this roadrunner has an oblong eye in a channel. However, other than this point, the two roadrunners are almost identical, including their silver stamps. It measures 1.06 inches tall and consists of blue turquoise, orange spiny oyster, spotted cowrie shell, white mother of pearl, and black jet.

Roadrunner pin, mosaic inlay, Pitkin Natewa, no hallmark, 1960s–70s, 1.93" x 0.73", $80–120.

Pitkin Natewa made this roadrunner pin in the mosaic inlay style in the 1960s or 1970s. It is somewhat similar to the preceding two roadrunners described. However, its wings are not evident in this design. It measures 0.73 inches tall and consists of blue turquoise, red coral, white mother of pearl, and dark brown tortoise shell.

Roadrunner tie tack, mosaic inlay, Gary and Paulinis Vacit, no hallmark, 1960s–70s, 1.46" x 0.68", $80–120.

Gary and Paulinis Vacit made this roadrunner tie tack in the mosaic inlay style in the 1960s or 1970s. It measures 0.68 inches tall. Considering this smaller size, the intricacy of their inlay work is incredible. It is made of blue turquoise, iridescent abalone, light brown tortoise shell, and black jet.

Roadrunner earrings, mosaic inlay, Gary and Paulinis Vacit(?), no hallmark, 1950s–60s, 0.91" x 0.76", $120–180.

Roadrunner pin, mosaic inlay, Ellen Quandelacy, no hallmark, 1950s–60s, 2.52" x 1.51", $200–300.

Roadrunner earrings, mosaic inlay, Ellen Quandelacy, 1950s–60s, no hallmark, roadrunners 1.10" x 0.63", $200–300.

The same couple probably made these roadrunner earrings, done in the mosaic inlay style in the 1950s or 1960s. It measures 0.76 inches tall. Considering this measurement, the intricacy of their inlay work is far beyond anything we could imagine. It consists of blue turquoise, iridescent abalone, and black jet.

Ellen Quandelacy made this Roadrunner pin in the channel inlay style in the 1950s or 1960s. A nearly identical pin is in *Zuni: The Art and the People* Vol. 2 (Bell and others, 1976, p.44). It measures 1.51 inches tall and consists of blue/green Kingman turquoise and black jet.

The same artist made these roadrunner earrings in the mosaic inlay style in the 1950s or 1960s. They are similar to the aforementioned roadrunner pin. Except for their black jet eyes, they are made solely with green Blue Gem turquoise. The roadrunners measure 0.63 inches tall each.

Owls are frequently carved as fetishes and often created in jewelry as well. In the C. G. Wallace Auction Catalogue, two owl pins made by Theodore Edaakie are featured; one of them was made in 1932 (#1046).

As to the meanings of owl, Kent McManis (1995) notes:

> To Native Americans, owls are somewhat like anchovies. You either love them or hate them. Some Native American groups perceive owls as harbingers of death, while others may see them as guardians of both the home and the village, hooting to warn villagers of approaching enemies. (p. 25)

Owl bolo, mosaic inlay, Theodore and Margaret Edaakie, no hallmark, 1950s–60s, 2.23" x 2.79", $1000-1500.

Theodore and Margaret Edaakie made this owl bolo in the mosaic inlay style in the 1950s or 1960s. This motif almost always accompanies a crescent moon and star. This particular design is featured in the *Arizona Highways: Hall of Fame Classics Edition* (August 1974, p. 45), two examples of which have horizontally extended horns, while the following two bolos have erected horns. Their smaller owl pieces always have these kinds of horizontally extended horns. The silver stamps all around the owl and stamped silver drops are the same as the ones seen in their roadrunners. It measures 2.79 inches tall and consists of blue turquoise, red coral, iridescent abalone, dark brown tortoise shell, white mother of pearl, and black jet.

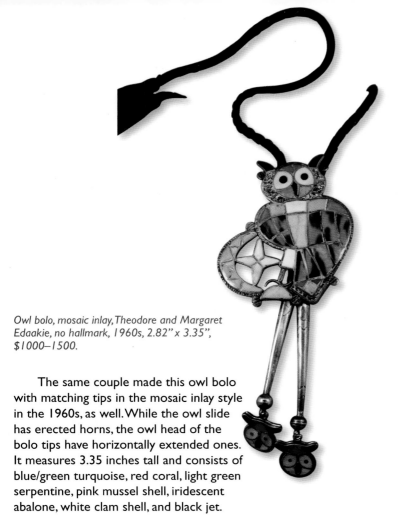

Owl bolo, mosaic inlay, Theodore and Margaret Edaakie, no hallmark, 1960s, 2.82" x 3.35", $1000–1500.

The same couple made this owl bolo with matching tips in the mosaic inlay style in the 1960s, as well. While the owl slide has erected horns, the owl head of the bolo tips have horizontally extended ones. It measures 3.35 inches tall and consists of blue/green turquoise, red coral, light green serpentine, pink mussel shell, iridescent abalone, white clam shell, and black jet.

Owl bolo, mosaic inlay, Theodore and Margaret Edaakie, TE, 1970s–80s, 3.00" x 3.54", $1000–1500.

Theodore and Margaret also made this owl bolo with matching tips in the 1970s or 1980s in the mosaic inlay style. As it has their hallmark, "TE," stamped on a small silver platelet and welded on its back, it was, without any doubt, made by them. Like the previous bolo, this slide has erected horns. It measures 3.54 inches tall and consists of blue/green turquoise, red coral, purple lip mother of pearl, gold lip mother of pearl, green serpentine, dark brown tortoise shell, white mother of pearl, and black jet.

Owl bracelet, mosaic inlay, Theodore and Margaret Edaakie, TE, 1970s–80s, 2.78" x 2.44", $1000–1500.

Also in the 1970s or 1980s, the Edaakies made this owl bracelet in the mosaic inlay style. It has a hallmark identical to the bolo just described, above. The owl has horizontally extended horns and is accompanied by a crescent moon and star on its right side, and a crescent moon and round red star on its left side. These are all set flush except for two coral cabochons on silver leaves set on both sides of its head. Stamped silver edges around the owl and stamped silver drops are identical to those seen in Theodore and Margaret's roadrunner pieces. The owl measures 2.44 inches tall and consists of blue/green turquoise, red coral, gold lip mother of pearl, yellow clam shell, dark brown pen shell, white mother of pearl, and black jet.

Owl ring, mosaic inlay, Theodore and Margaret Edaakie, TE, 1970s–80s, 1.43" x 1.63", $200–300.

The Edaakies also made this owl ring in the 1970s or 1980s in the mosaic inlay style. It has Theodore and Margaret's hallmark on its back. It has horizontally extended horns, and a crescent moon and round star on its right side, all of which are similar to those decorations on the bracelet. It measures 1.63 inches tall and consists of blue/green turquoise, red coral, purple lip mother of pearl, gold lip mother of pearl, brown pen shell, white mother of pearl, and black jet.

Owl ring, mosaic inlay, Theodore and Margaret Edaakie, no hallmark, 1950s–60s, 1.03" x 1.47", $160–240.

Owl pendant, mosaic inlay, Theodore and Margaret Edaakie, no hallmark, 1950s–60s, 0.99" x 0.91", $100–150.

Opposite:
Owl bolo, mosaic inlay, Velma and Blake Lesansee,, V. Lesansee, 1980s, 0.94" x 1.91", $160–240.

This is another owl ring by Theodore and Margaret Edaakie, made in the mosaic inlay style in the 1950s or 1960s. It is identical to the owl ring just described, above, except that it lacks a crescent moon and silver stamps around its edges. It measures 1.47 inches tall and consists of blue/green turquoise, red coral, dark brown tortoise shell, white mother of pearl, and black jet.

Also in the 1950s or 1960s, the couple made this owl pendant in the mosaic inlay style. This might have been converted from an earring or bolo tip. It is similar to the bolo tips seen in their second and third owl bolos. It measures 0.91 inches tall and consists of green turquoise, red coral, spotted cowrie shell, white mother of pearl, and black jet.

Velma and Blake Lesansee made this owl bolo in the mosaic inlay style in the 1980s. Their owl design is similar to that made by Pitkin Natewa and Allyn and Verna Zunie, but also somewhat different. The head and horns on Velma and Blake's owl are crescent shaped, on Pitkin's they are circular and almost oblong, and on Allyn and Virna's they are triangular. In addition, Verna and Blake always use different colors of stones/shells for each owl's chest and tail. Its belly and tail are set a bit higher than its face and chest. It measures 1.91 inches tall and consists of blue turquoise, red coral, spotted cowrie shell, white mother of pearl, and black jet.

Owl bolo, mosaic inlay, artist unknown, no hallmark, 1940s–50s, 2.89" x 2.91", $400–600.

Owl pin, mosaic inlay, artist unknown, no hallmark, 1940s–60s, 1.07" x 1.67", $150-225.

An unknown artist made this owl bolo in the raised mosaic inlay style in the 1940s or 1950s. One informant of mine was not sure of the artist, and another informant attributed it to Oliver Cellicion. It is a huge bolo, measuring 2.91 inches tall. The bolo slide has two U-shaped silver platelets for clasps. On the back, there is a mark of a small dumb-bell-like sticker. It consists of blue/green turquoise, red coral, white and orange clam shell, and dark brown tortoise shell.

This is an owl pin by the same artist, made in the raised mosaic inlay style in the 1940s or 1960s. One of my informants attributed it to Elliot Qualo. The design is rare—I have seen only two examples so far. Its white chest and belly are set a bit higher than the remaining area. It measures 1.67 inches tall and consists of blue turquoise, brown tortoise shell, and white mother of pearl.

5 Quails

Quails have been made often in Zuni jewelry. Leonard and Edith Lonjose, Elliot Qualo, and Porfilio and Ann Sheyka are famous for their quail designs in Zuni jewelry.

Quail bird bolo, mosaic inlay, Juan Qualo Jr., no hallmark, 1940s–50s, 1.83" x 3.21", $400–600.

Juan Qualo Jr. made this quail bolo in the 1950s or 1960s in the mosaic inlay style. Although one of my informants attributed it to Elliot Qualo, it was confirmed as Juan's by his wife, Marie, and her daughter, whose name I am not sure of. It is large and bold, especially in its stamp work. Its wing is set higher than the remaining area, which is set flush. It measures 3.21 inches tall and consists of green turquoise, red coral, brown tortoise shell, moss green/light brown Zuni rock, and iridescent abalone shell.

Opposite: Bobwhite quail bird bolo with matching tips, mosaic inlay, Porfilio and Ann Sheyka, P and Sheyka 78, 1978, 2.55" x 3.69", $2000–3000.

Porfilio and Ann Sheyka made this bobwhite quail bolo with matching quail head tips in the mosaic inlay style in 1978. It has their P hallmark on a small silver platelet, and "Sheyka 78" is etched with an electric pencil. There are etchings all over its body that give this bird a realistic look. Its belly is set higher than the remaining area. However, the area is not set flush, but individually cut, polished, etched, and then set. The bird stands still on the rocks. It is a one-of-a-kind piece. It measures 3.69 inches tall and consists of dark brown pen shell, spotted cowrie shell, gold lip mother of pearl, iridescent abalone, and white mother of pearl.

Quail bird bolo, mosaic inlay, Porfilio and Ann Sheyka, P and Sheyka, 1980s, 1.12" x 1.62", $400–600.

Quail bird pendant, mosaic inlay, Porfilio and Ann Sheyka, P and Sheyka, 1980s, 1.19" x 1.66", $200–300.

In the 1980s, the couple also made this quail bolo in the mosaic inlay style. It has their P hallmark on a small silver platelet and "Sheyka" on its back, manually etched using an electric pencil. Stone and shell parts seem to be carved, etched, polished, and then set individually in each channel. It measures 1.62 inches tall and consists of green turquoise, red coral, dark brown pen shell, white mother of pearl, and black jet.

This is a quail pendant by Porfilio and Ann Sheyka, made in the mosaic inlay style in the 1980s. It has their P hallmark on a small silver platelet and "Sheyka" on its back, manually etched using an electric pencil. It measures 1.66 inches tall and consists of green turquoise, red coral, dark brown pen shell, white mother of pearl, and black jet.

Quail bird pendant, mosaic inlay, Effie Qualo, Effie Qualo, 1980s, 2.23" in diameter, $200–300.

Quail bird pin/pendant, mosaic inlay, Deann Qualo, no hallmark, 2009, 0.61" x 1.40", $80–120.

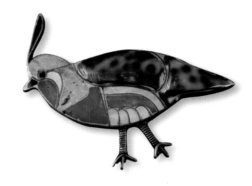

Quail bird pin, mosaic inlay, artist unknown, W inside of large O, 1950s–60s, 2.11" x 1.87", $400–600.

Effie Qualo made this quail pin/pendant, in the mosaic inlay in abalone shell style in the 1990s. It was presented to me by my friend and potter, Randy Nahohai. It was made in the same style used by her late husband, Elliot Qualo. Her design of the quail is not so intricate as the one made by Elliot. The bird, the scenery, and the background are all set flush, except for the red wing. It measures 2.23 inches in diameter and consists of blue turquoise, red coral, iridescent abalone, gold lip mother of pearl, and black lip mother of pearl.

Deann Qualo made this quail pin/pendant in 2009 in the mosaic inlay style. Deann is a daughter of Juan Qualo Jr. and Marie Qualo. The wing of the quail is set higher than the remaining area. This characteristic is common among the quails made by Elliot, Effie, Juan, and Deann. It measures 1.40 inches tall and consists of blue turquoise, red coral, grey serpentine, and dark brown pen shell.

An unknown artist made this quail pin in the mosaic inlay style in the 1950s-1960s. The back and the tail of the bird are set higher than the remaining area. While almost all quails made by other artists are vertically long, this bird is made horizontally long. It measures 1.87 inches tall and consists of blue/green turquoise, red coral, spotted cowrie shell, white mother of pearl, and black jet.

Here, I am going to introduce other, less frequently utilized birds from the 1940s to the 1960s. They are phoenix birds, red birds, blue birds, hummingbirds, peacocks, parrots, and pheasants.

Phoenix Bird bolo,
mosaic inlay,
Dixon Shebola, no hallmark,
1950s–60s, 2.94" x 3.51",
$1000–1500.

Dixon Shebola made this phoenix bird bolo in the mosaic inlay style in the 1950s or 1960s. The owner of the Inn at the Halona in Zuni, Roger Thomas, once showed me a similar phoenix bird pin, which is also identical to the one from the Visitor's Guide section of *The Spirit of Zuni* (2005, p. VG2). Its caption says, "Weahkee." This bolo was confirmed as Dixon's by his brother, Milford Nahohai. The wings get closer to its head and the central feather of its tail has a round point. In addition, we can notice black feet under its tail and its thighs are set under its chest. Its chest and hands are set higher than the remaining area. It measures 3.51 inches tall and consists of blue/green turquoise, red coral, white mother of pearl, and black jet.

Phoenix Bird bolo, mosaic inlay, Dixon Shebola, no hallmark, 1950s–60s, 2.98" x 3.51", $1000–1500.

Around the same time, the same artist made this nearly identical Phoenix bird bolo in the same style. Its chest and hands are set higher than the remaining area. It measures 3.51 inches tall and consists of blue/green turquoise, orange coral, white mother of pearl, and black jet.

Phoenix Bird pin, mosaic inlay, Tom Weahkee, CW, 1970s, 1.97" x 2.02", $400–600.

Tom Weahkee is likely responsible for this phoenix bird pin made in the raised mosaic inlay in mother of pearl shell style in the 1970s. Its attribution is made in part because its characteristics are identical to those observed in Roger Thomas's pin. Its wings do not get closer to its head, and the central feather of its tail has a sharp point. In addition, its turquoise thighs are set in the chest. Its chest, hands, and thighs are set higher than the remaining area of its body. The phoenix bird itself measures 1.17 inches tall, while the pin measures 2.02 inches tall. Considering this small size, Weahkee's lapidary skill can be called truly incredible. It consists of blue turquoise, red coral, white mother of pearl, and black jet.

Phoenix Bird bracelet, mosaic inlay, Lambert Homer Jr.(?), no hallmark, 1950s–60s, central medallion 2.69" x 2.40", $800–1200.

Lambert Homer Jr. probably made this phoenix bird bracelet, from the 1950s or 1960s, which is in the mosaic inlay style. On the circular, oblong base, the channel walls of the phoenix design are set and edge walls are constructed. Then, the bird is inlaid with green turquoise, white mother of pearl, and black jet. Lastly, the background is inlaid with various shades of green turquoise. The medallion measures 2.40 inches tall.

Bird bracelet, mosaic inlay, Theodore and Margaret Edaakie, TE, 1970s–80s, central medallion 1.67" x 1.50", $800–1200.

Bird bolo, mosaic inlay in mother of pearl, Homer and Myra Vacit, no hallmark, 1940s–50s, 1.98" x 1.92", $1200–1800.

Homer and Myra Vacit made this bird bolo in the mosaic inlay in mother of pearl shell style in the 1940s or 1950s. A rectangular and concaved shell is cut out to create a bird-and-tree-branch design in which stone, shell, and silver strip parts are inlaid. This insert is set on the silver backing using silver bezel. Oblong, stamped silver drops are set around the insert on the silver backing. It measures 1.92 inches tall and consists of green turquoise, red coral, and silver and black jet in the figural designs, and white mother of pearl in the background.

In the 1970s or 1980s, Theodore and Margaret Edaakie made this bird bracelet in the mosaic inlay style. The construction of this bracelet is extremely complex. The twisted and flattened silver wires are set in the lowest layer around the central medallion. In the second lowest layer, two sets of three half-circular stones are set on each side of the medallion. In the third lowest layer, a round background is then set in the center, where a bird and wreath are set on the top layer. It consists of blue/green turquoise, red coral, white clam shell, white mother of pearl, and black jet, and the central medallion measures 1.50 inches.

Blue jay bolo, mosaic inlay, Frank and Elizabeth Vacit, no hallmark, 1940s–50s, 2.14" x 1.97", $1200–1800.

Blue bird and flower pin, mosaic inlay, Corraine Lesansee (Shack), no hallmark, 1950s–60s, 1.14" x 2.54", $200–300.

Hummingbird pin, mosaic inlay, Blake and Velma Lesansee, no hallmark, 1950s–60s, 1.89" x 1.77", $200–300.

Frank and Elizabeth Vacit made this blue bird bolo in the 1940s or 1950s in the mosaic inlay style. The bird perches on a branch and is about to peck something. Its tail, constructed intricately, is set a little lower than the body. It measures 1.97 inches tall and consists of blue/green turquoise, orange spiny oyster, white mother of pearl, and black jet.

Corraine Lesansee (Shack) made this blue bird and flower pin in the mosaic inlay style in the 1950s or 1960s. On the top of the gigantic flower, a little blue bird perches. The petals of the flower are inlaid with two different materials: white mother of pearl and abalone. It measures 2.54 inches tall and consists of blue/green turquoise, red coral, white mother of pearl, iridescent abalone, and dark brown tortoise shell.

In the 1950s or 1960s, Blake and Velma Lesansee made this hummingbird pin in the mosaic inlay style. The bird is hovering in the sky and trying to suck the nectar of the flower, signified by a stamped silver drop. It measures 1.77 inches tall and consists of blue turquoise, red coral, spotted cowrie shell, and iridescent abalone.

Peacock bolo, mosaic inlay, Walter Nakatewa, no hallmark, 1940s–50s, 2.15" x 2.03", $800–1200.

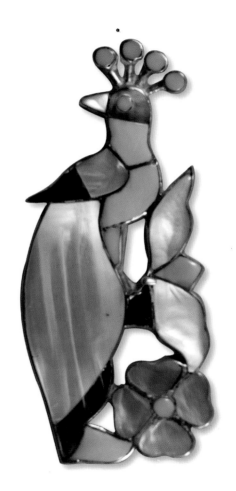

Peacock pin/pendant, mosaic inlay, Jack Mahke, J. Mahke, 1980s–90s, 0.97" x 2.24", $200–300.

Walter Nakatewa made this peacock bolo in the mosaic inlay style in the 1940s or 1950s. It has two U-shaped silver platelets for a bolo clasp. It is made in a simple, old-style design, and so, cannot have been made in the 1960s or thereafter. To me, it's extremely attractive. It measures 2.03 inches tall and consists of blue/green turquoise, orange spiny oyster, white clam shell, and black jet.

Jack Mahke made this peacock pin/ pendant in the 1980s or 1990s in the mosaic inlay style. It looks much more modern than the peacock bolo just described, above. It perches on a branch with flowers and looks back in another direction. It looks natural. There are some carvings in its wings and in its long tail. It measures 2.24 inches tall and consists of blue turquoise, white mother of pearl, and brown and black lip mother of pearl.

The following three pieces are Parrots.
In Zuni there is a parrot clan, and parrot
feathers have been used for the adornment
of the regalia of the religious dancers.

*Parrot and Sun Face bolo,
mosaic inlay, Rosemary Cellicion,
no hallmark, 1940s–50s,
2.55" x 2.90", $2000–3000.*

*Parrot ring, mosaic inlay,
artist unknown, no
hallmark, 1960s–70s,
0.93" x 1.55", $120–180.*

*Parrot necklace, silver overlay and mosaic inlay,
Dennis and Nancy Edaakie, Dennis Nancy Edaakie,
2000s, 3.70" x 2.38", $600–900.*

An unknown artist made this parrot ring in the mosaic inlay style in the 1960s or 1970s. It perches on a branch, and there are etchings all over its body, wings, tail, and crest. It measures 1.55 inches tall and consists of pink mussel shell and white mother of pearl. This scarcity of colors is rarely seen.

Dennis and Nancy Edaakie made this parrot necklace in the 2000s in the silver overlay and mosaic inlay style. This innovation of realistic birds in silver overlay and mosaic inlay is their invention. It measures 2.38 inches tall and consists of blue turquoise, red coral, black lip mother of pearl, and iridescent abalone.

Rosemary Cellicion made this double parrot over Sun Father bolo in the mosaic inlay style in the 1940s or 1950s. This design is extremely rare, and may be a derivative of the Sun Father and his Sons design (Sei, 2011, pp. 136-140). It is not naturalistic, but decorative. Each part is individually formed, cut, and set into channels. On the eagle feathers of the Sun Father, there are black dots in the white bodies, which are rare in bird motifs. Also rare is the black and white bridge over the parrots' heads. It measures 2.90 inches tall and consists of blue/green turquoise, red coral, white mother of pearl, and black jet.

Pheasant necklace, mosaic inlay, Porfilio Sheyka, P and Sheyka, 1970s–80s, 2.95" x 1.90", $1000–1500.

Three of the following four fetish jewelry pieces are made by members of the Leekya family.

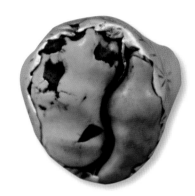

Bird Ring, carving, artist unknown, no hallmark, 1940s–50s, 0.54" x 1.52", $300–450.

In the 1970s or 1980s, Porfilio and Ann Sheyka made this pheasant necklace in the mosaic inlay style. It is a realistic and well-made piece. It appears to be a flush inlay, but each piece is cut, polished, and set individually in channels. There are intricate etching lines on its chest, wing, and back. Its face and tail are set slightly higher than the remaining area. It measures 1.90 inches tall and consists of blue turquoise, red coral, dark brown pen shell, spotted cowrie shell, gold lip mother of pearl, iridescent abalone, and orange shell.

Bird Ring, carving, Leekya Deyuse, no hallmark, 1940s–50s, 0.79" x 0.96", $2000–3000.

Leekya Deyuse carved and set this turquoise bird ring in the 1940s or 1950s. It features his signature roundness and smoothness. The slim carving is apparently a bird, and the other might be a rock. It was originally sold as Teddy Weahkee piece but it turned out to be an older Leekya piece. It measures 0.96 inches tall.

An unknown artist made this carved bird ring in the 1940s or 1950s. As soon as I found it in an online auction, I got it without hesitation, because it appears to be an authentic Zuni carving to me. In response to my question about its attribution, my Facebook friend, Kent McManis, could not identify the original artist, but did not consider it to be Leekya's. He agreed with me that the piece is an authentic Zuni carving. It measures 1.52 inches long and is made with white mother of pearl.

Bird pendant, carving, Sarah Leekya, no hallmark, 1960s–70s, 1.23" x 0.85", $120–180.

Bird ring, carving, Sarah Leekya, no hallmark, 1960s–70s, 1.31" x 0.48", $100–150.

Sarah Leekya made this carved shell bird pendant in the 1960s or 1970s. It measures 0.85 inches tall.

She also made this carved bird ring around the same time. I got it in an online auction, not knowing who made it. It measures 0.48 inches tall.

In total, I have included more than seventy bird pieces here. Roadrunners make up the largest portion, and owls and eagles total ten each. Here, I would like to comment on the husband and wife team, Theodore and Margaret Edaakie. Their roadrunners and owls are included in the C. G. Wallace Auction Catalogue and are represented the most in this bird chapter. As shown in both the owls and roadrunners sections, their pieces always show variation, even if the motifs are identical.

Eagles almost always have one snake in their feet while owls do not, except for the owl made by Porfilio and Ann Sheyka, which I do not own.

≡ IV ≡

Domesticated Animals

The *C. G. Wallace Auction Catalogue* features seventeen domestic animals. Out of these, eight are made in the mosaic inlay style. They include six horses or horse heads, one cow, and one burro. They were probably made, for the most part, in the 1920s or 1930s. To me, this estimated time of production seems too early. Of these eight pieces, three are made by Walter Nakatewa, two by Sam Poblano, and one each by Leonard Martza, Juan de Dios, and an unknown artist.

The January 1945 issue of Arizona Highways includes no domesticated animals, but the August 1952 issue includes a horse or donkey with a covered wagon pin, and a sweater guard of a tree with a horse or donkey. The August 1959 issue includes horse head and steer head tie bars, which are probably made by one of the Zunie brothers—Lincoln or Joe. I would say that domesticated animals were made sporadically in the 1940s and more frequently in the 1950s.

1 Horses

Domesticated animals total more than twenty pieces, including fourteen horses.

Here, I would like to briefly discuss the similarity of designs among horses made by Dan Simplicio, Chauncy and Isabel Simplicio, and Elliot Qualo. There is no doubt about the similarity of the designs between Dan and Chauncy, because they are brothers, and Dan taught Chauncy how to do silver and lapidary work. However, it is surprising to see the apparent similarities in the designs made by Dan Simplicio and Elliot Qualo. It goes without saying that Dan and Elliot's pieces are the best.

There are eight horse pieces in the C. G. Wallace Auction Catalogue, two of which are carvings set on silver by Leekya Deyuse. Out of the remaining six pieces, two pieces each were made by Walter Nakatewa and by Sam Poblano, and one each was made by Leonard Martza and by an unknown artist.

Horse head bolo with matching tips, mosaic inlay, Nora Leekity, no hallmark, 1940s–50s, 2.00" x 1.91", $600–900.

Nora Leekity made this horse head bolo with matching tips in the mosaic inlay style in the 1940s or 1950s. She is famous for her horses, and has been active since the 1940s. It features her signature round eye and nostril. She cut, polished, and set all parts individually into the channels. Consequently, her mosaic inlay looks somewhat three dimensional. The slide measures 1.91 inches tall and consists of blue/green turquoise, red spiny oyster, white mother of pearl, and black jet.

Horse head bolo with matching tips, mosaic inlay, Nora Leekity, no hallmark, 1940s–50s, 1.17" x 1.34", $300–450.

The same artist also made this horse head bolo in the mosaic inlay style around the same time. Although its ears and mane are sharper than those just described, above, the remaining parts, including the silver work, are almost identical. It measures 1.34 inches tall and consists of blue turquoise, orange spiny oyster, white mother of pearl, and black jet.

Appaloosa horse bolo with matching tips, raised mosaic inlay with etching, Joe Zunie, Joe Zuni and JZJ, 1980s, 3.62" x 2.95", $1200–1800.

Horse bolo, mosaic inlay, Nora Leekity, Nora Leekity, 1960s–80s, 2.48" x 1.99", $500–750.

Horse head bolo, mosaic inlay, Lincoln Zunie, no hallmark, 1950s, 1.50" x 1.47", $500–750.

In the 1960s or 1980s, she made this horse bolo in the same style. This is her standard horse bolo design frequently seen on the market. It is made in flush inlay except for its back hip. Its front left leg is always raised and bent. This pose gives the figure a feeling of motion. It measures 1.99 inches tall and consists of blue turquoise, black lip mother of pearl, spotted cowrie shell, white mother of pearl, and dark brown pen shell.

Lincoln and Helen Zunie made this horse head bolo in the mosaic inlay style in the 1950s. The shape of its eye is characteristic of their works. All parts are inlaid flush. In addition, each bolo tip is set with a smaller turquoise cabochon, which enhances this bolo's attractiveness. It measures 1.47 inches tall and consists of blue/green turquoise, orange abalone, black jet, and coiled silver wires.

In the 1980s Joe Zunie made this appaloosa horse bolo with matching tips in the mosaic inlay style. It has the hallmarks Joe Zuni and JZJ. Some parts, including tail, mane, and saddle, are set higher than the horse's body, and there are etchings placed all over the horse. Its front right leg is bent and raised very high. This pose gives the horse a strong sense of motion. The rocks and glass under its feet are characteristic of Joe's animal figures, including wild ones. It measures 2.95 inches tall and consists of blue turquoise, orange coral, white mother of pearl, and dark brown pen shell.

Horse bolo, raised mosaic inlay with etching, Dan Simplicio, no hallmark, 1950s–60s, 2.05" x 2.59", $1200–1800.

Dan Simplicio made this horse head bolo in the 1950s or 1960s in the mosaic inlay style. This attribution is confirmed by Dan's son, Dan Simplicio Jr. The horse head is set a little bit higher than the surface of the background, and the colorful red and green bridles stand out. Its upper half is etched like a real mane. The bezels and stamped silver edge all around the insert are reminiscent of Elliot Qualo's horse, but Simplicio's is still quite different from Qualo's. This silver stamp looks like a chain of bow shapes. It measures 2.59 inches tall and consists of green turquoise, red coral, white mother of pearl, black pigment, and dark brown pen shell.

Horse bolo, mosaic inlay in mother of pearl shell, Dan Simplicio, no hallmark, 1950s–60s, 1.70" x 2.23", $1200–1800.

Around the same time, Dan made this horse head bolo in the mosaic inlay in mother of pearl shell style. The two stamped silver drops and three stamped silver leaves apparently confirm it as Dan's. Although this horse head design is very similar to the one made by Isabelle and Chauncy Simplicio, the tuft of hair in front of the ears is the distinguishing factor. It measures 2.23 inches tall and consists of tortoise shell, mother of pearl, and silver platelet.

Horse head bolo, mosaic inlay in tortoise shell, Elliot Qualo, no hallmark, 1940s–50s, 1.68" across, $600–900.

Elliot Qualo made this horse head bolo in the mosaic inlay in tortoise shell style in the 1940s or 1950s. These bezels and stamps around the insert are also observed in his Knifewing pieces (Sei, 2010, pp. 130-131). The horse head is etched all over including its eye, nose, and mouth, and black pigment is placed in them. Its bridles are inlaid with silver threads. It measures 1.27 inches in diameter and consists of white mother of pearl, silver thread, black pigment, and dark brown tortoise shell.

Horse head pin, mosaic inlay in tortoise shell, Elliot Qualo, no hallmark, 1950s–60s, 1.76" x 1.27", $600–900.

In the 1950s or 1960s, Elliot made this double horse head pin in the same style. The horse design is identical to the one just described, above. The bezels and silver stamps are identical to the ones seen in his other pieces. Consequently, we can safely say this pin is Elliot's. It measures 1.27 inches tall and consists of white mother of pearl, silver threads, black pigment, and dark brown tortoise shell.

Horse cufflinks, mosaic inlay in mother of pearl, Elliot Qualo, no hallmark, 1970s–80s, 0.92" across, $300–450.

These horse head cufflinks by the same artist were made in the mosaic inlay in mother of pearl shell style, also in the 1950s or 1960s. Although dark brown and white are reversed, the horse head design, bezels, and stamped silver edge are consistent with his other work. It measures 0.92 inches in diameter and consists of dark brown pen shell, silver threads, and white mother of pearl.

Horse head bolo, mosaic inlay in mother of pearl with etching and nugget work, Leonard Martza, LM, 2007, 2.43" across, $400–600.

In 2007, Leonard Martza made this horse head bolo in the mosaic inlay style in a mother of pearl background. The horse head is set higher than the surface of the mother of pearl background, like a relief, encircled by thirteen turquoise cabochons. Its neck is etched to show its mane. It measures 2.43 inches in diameter and consists of blue turquoise, dark brown pen shell, and white mother of pearl.

Horse head bolo with horse shoe, mosaic inlay with etching, Virgil and Shirley Benn, Virgil and Shirley Benn handwritten, 1968, 1.41" x 1.40", $600–900.

Virgil and Shirley Benn made this horse head and shoe bolo in the mosaic inlay style in the 1960s or 1980s. There are etchings all over its head. It is a well-conceived and well-made piece—their creativity exceeds that of many contemporary artists. It measures 1.40 inches tall and consists of blue turquoise, red coral, black lip mother of pearl, white mother of pearl, and black jet.

Appaloosa horse bolo, mosaic inlay with etching, Jack Mahkee, J. Mahkee handwritten, 1970s–80s, 2.93" x 3.02", $600–900.

This Appaloosa horse bolo by Jack Mahke was made in the 1970s or 1980s in the mosaic inlay style. It is carved in its mane and tail. Some parts are set higher than others. It measures 3.02 inches tall and consists of blue turquoise, spotted cowrie shell, green serpentine, turtle shell, white mother of pearl, black jet, and yellow shell.

Horse bolo, mosaic inlay in Pen shell and nugget work, Isabel and Chauncy Simplicio, no hallmark, 1980s–90s, 1.12" x 1.36", $200–300.

Isabel and Chauncy Simplicio made this horse head bolo in the mosaic inlay in pen shell style in the 1980s or 1990s. The insert itself measures 0.75 inches in diameter. Considering its smaller size, their lapidary skill is quite incredible. In addition, there are stamps all over the silver backing, and stamped silver drops are set among them. The slide measures 1.36 inches tall and consists of blue turquoise, white mother of pearl, dark brown pen shell, and black pigment.

The C. G. Wallace Auction Catalogue includes seven steers and a cow. The cow, made by Walter Nakatewa, is the only piece of mosaic jewelry. One steer bracelet is made by Juan de Dios in the silver cast work, and the remaining six steers are carvings made by Leekya Deyuse.

Steer head ring, carving, Leekya Deyuse, no hallmark, 1940s, 0.82" x 0.69", $2400–3600.

Leekya Deyuse carved and set this steer head ring in the 1940s. It used to be in the heirloom collection of Alice Leekya Homer and Leekya's extended family. Its roundness and smoothness are obviously characteristics of the Leekya's work. Its nostrils, ear holes, and mouth are carved in, and its black jet eyes are inlaid. The two stamps on the side of the ring have features reminiscent of the 1940s, as well. The steer head measures 0.69 inches long from mouth to head.

Side view of the Steer Head ring made by Leekya Deyuse.

Cow bolo, mosaic inlay, artist unknown, no hallmark, 1940s–50s, 2.41" x 2.18", $1000–1500.

Steer head bolo, mosaic inlay, Joe Zunie, no hallmark, 1950s–60s, 2.34" x 1.68", $600–900.

Steer head bolo with matching tips, mosaic inlay with etching, Joe Zuni handwritten, 1968, 2.43" x 2.47", $800–1200.

In the 1940s or 1950s, Dan Simplicio probably made this cow head bolo, done in the mosaic inlay style. Although the moving part of the clasp has the mark "Bennett Pat. Pend. C31," due to of the presence of the welding marks, it's possible that this part was attached later. One of my informants attributed it to Joe Zunie, but Dan Simplicio Jr. told me it could be his father's. It is a well-conceived and well-executed cow bolo. Each part is individually carved, polished, and set into channels. This technique gives it a three-dimensional effect. It measures 2.18 inches tall and consists of blue turquoise, black lip mother of pearl, orange coral, orange clam shell, and iridescent abalone.

Joe Zunie made this steer Head bolo in the mosaic inlay style in the 1950s or 1960s. Although Joe Zunie is said only to have been active since 1960, this bolo has a hand-made, double-wire clasp, an old-style technique that isn't commonly believed to have survived into the '60s, but may have nonetheless. It has a characteristic form of eye, which is different from the one made by his brother, Lincoln Zunie, and has unique tips with turquoise. There is no etching on this piece, unlike Joe's later pieces. It measures 1.68 inches tall and consists of blue turquoise, red spiny oyster, white mother of pearl, and black jet.

In the 1960s, Joe Zunie made this steer head bolo in the mosaic inlay style. It has an eye characteristic to Joe's style and etchings all over. His hallmark, "by Joe Zuni", is written with an electric pencil. It measures 2.47 inches tall and consists of blue turquoise, red spiny oyster, iridescent abalone, white mother of pearl, and black jet.

Steer head buckle, mosaic inlay, Nora Leekity, Nora Leekity Zuni, 1970s–80s, steer head 2.29" x 1.74", $600–900.

Steer head bolo, mosaic inlay, Helen and Lincoln Zunie, no hallmark, 1950s–60s, 2.40" x 2.13", $600–900.

Cow bolo, mosaic inlay, Nora Leekity, no hallmark, 1960s, 2.08" x 1.71", $400–600.

This steer head bolo by Helen and Lincoln Zunie was made in the mosaic inlay style in the 1950s or 1960s. Its eyes, tender in appearance, are different from those made by his brother, Joe Zunie. There are etchings all over its face. It measures 2.13 inches tall and consists of orange spiny oyster, white mother of pearl, and black pigment.

In the 1970s or 1980s Nora Leekity made this steer head buckle in the mosaic inlay style. All parts which construct the steer head are individually formed, polished, and set into channels. This technique gives it a three-dimensional effect. Three oblong turquoise cabochons are set in the empty corners of the buckle, and flower-like stamps are placed all over the remaining area. The steer head and the buckle measure 1.74 and 2.02 inches tall, respectively, and consists of blue turquoise, orange abalone, white mother of pearl, and black jet.

This cow bolo by Nora Leekity was made in the 1960s in the mosaic inlay style. Although her hallmark does not appear on the back, it is obviously her work. Each part of the cow is formed, polished, and set into channels. This technique gives it a three-dimensional effect. It measures 1.71 inches tall and consists of blue turquoise, red abalone, white mother of pearl and black jet.

3 | Other Domesticated Animals

Other domesticated animals, such as dogs and cats, are rarely made in Zuni jewelry or in Zuni fetish carving.

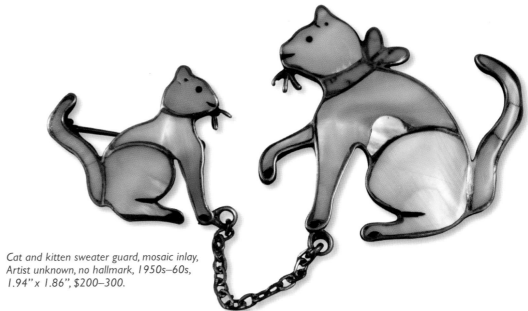

Cat and kitten sweater guard, mosaic inlay, Artist unknown, no hallmark, 1950s–60s, 1.94" x 1.86", $200–300.

An unknown Artist made this cat and kitten sweater guard in the mosaic inlay style in the 1950s or 1960s. Small jet parts are inlaid in the tips of their feet, and black pigment is placed in their etched eyes and ears. This is a rare, well-conceived, and well-executed piece. A master inlayer such as Shirley Benn could have made it. The mother cat measures 1.86 inches tall and consists of blue turquoise, white mother of pearl, and black jet.

≡ V ≡

Wild Animals

The *C. G. Wallace Auction Catalogue* includes twenty-one wild animal pieces. Ten of these are inlay, not carved, pieces. The identifiable artists of these ten pieces are Walter Nakatewa, Juan de Dios, Annie Quam Gasper, Lee Edaakie, and Teddy Weahkee.

The August 1952 issue of *Arizona Highways* includes a deer and tree sweater guard. The January 1945 and August 1959 issues contain no wild animal pieces.

1 Big Horn Sheep or Rams

There are two Ram bolos in the C. G. Wallace Auction Catalogue, but they are carvings by Leekya Deyuse. Consequently, there is no ram jewelry in the mosaic or channel inlay style in the catalog.

Rocky Mountain sheep bolo, mosaic inlay in tortoise shell, Elliot Qualo, double antlers, 1950s–60s, 2.76" across, $2000–3000.

Elliot Qualo made this Rocky Mountain sheep bolo in the 1950s or 1960s in the mosaic inlay in tortoise shell style. It features his double-antler hallmark, on its back, as well as his signature bezels and stamped edges. There are a lot of etchings all over sheep's body, the rocks, and the trees. It measures 2.76 inches in diameter and consists of blue/green turquoise, white mother of pearl, black jet, and dark brown tortoise shell.

Big horn sheep bolo with matching tips, mosaic inlay with etching, Joe Zunie, no hallmark, 1960s, 2.81" x 2.52", $1000–1500.

Big horn sheep bust bolo with matching tips, mosaic inlay with etching, Joe Zunie, JZJ, 1970s–80s, 2.00" x 2.65", $500–750.

In the 1960s, Joe Zunie made this big horn sheep bolo in the mosaic inlay style. Although there is no hallmark on its back, it can apparently be identified as Joe's work based on the posture of the animal, etchings on its body, rock, grass, and gigantic hooves. It measures 2.52 inches tall and consists of blue turquoise, red coral, white mother of pearl, and black jet.

Joe Zunie also made this big horn sheep bust bolo in the mosaic inlay style in the 1970s or 1980s. It has matching, gigantic hooves for tips. The big horns are set higher than the remaining area, and many etchings are placed all over the bust and hooves. The slide measures 2.65 inches tall and consists of blue turquoise, gold lip mother of pearl, white mother of pearl, and black jet.

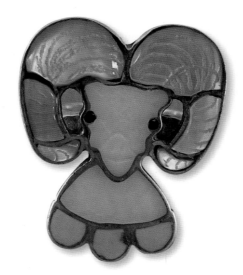

Big horn sheep bust ring, raised mosaic inlay with etching, Joe Zunie, JZJ, 1970s–80s, 1.06" x 1.31", $150–225.

Big horn sheep bust ring, raised mosaic inlay with etching, Joe Zunie, Joe Zuni, 1970s–80s, 1.13" x 1.43", $150–225.

Around the same time, the same artist also made this big horn sheep ring, in the same style. It matches the preceding bolo described. It measures 1.31 inches tall and consists of blue turquoise, gold lip mother of pearl, white mother of pearl, and black jet.

This may be a little bit older than the ring just described, above, because of the hallmark: "Joe Zuni." The horns are set higher than the remaining area, and there are etchings all over the body. It measures 1.43 inches tall and consists of red abalone, dark brown pen shell, white mother of pearl, and black jet.

There are seven pieces of deer jewelry in the C. G. Wallace Auction Catalogue. *Six of these are in mosaic or channel inlay, and only one is carved. As for these pieces, Walter Nakatewa, Annie Quam Gasper, and Lee Edaakie made one each, and the rest were made by unknown artists.*

Elk or deer bolo with matching tips, mosaic inlay with etching, Joe Zunie, JZJ, 1970s–80s, 2.97" x 2.81", $1000–1500.

Elk or deer pin, mosaic inlay with etching, Joe Zunie, no hallmark, 1960s, 2.49" x 3.29", $1200–1800.

In the 1970s or 1980s, Joe Zunie made this elk or deer bolo, in the mosaic inlay style. It is in exactly the same pose as his big horn sheep with matching hooves for tips. This bolo has matching hooves for tips as well. It is a flush inlay piece, but there are etchings all over its body. It measures 2.81 inches tall and consists of blue turquoise, red coral, brown pen shell, and gold lip mother of pearl.

Joe made this elk or deer pin, in the mosaic inlay style, in the 1960s. There is no hallmark on the back. Faint etchings suggest the animal's fur, and, typical of Joe's animal pieces, rocks and grass surround his feet. It stands still and calls his mate. It measures 3.29 inches tall and consists of blue turquoise, red coral, brown pen shell, gold lip mother of pearl, and black jet.

The antelope, or, prong-horn, has a pair of distinctive horns, and only one prong on each horn. It is a game animal for Pueblo people. There are a lot of Antelope dancers in the Buffalo Dance in many Pueblos. In Zuni, there is an Antelope Kachina in the religious dance, and it has been made frequently in jewelry. The antelope as game has been created frequently in jewelry, as well.

Antelope bolo, mosaic inlay, Elliot Qualo(?), no hallmark, 1940s–50s, 2.50" x 3.26", $2000–3000.

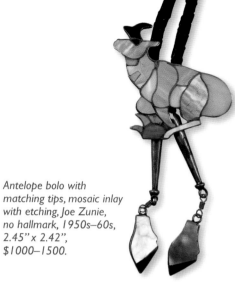

Antelope bolo with matching tips, mosaic inlay with etching, Joe Zunie, no hallmark, 1950s–60s, 2.45" x 2.42", $1000–1500.

Elliot Qualo is probably responsible for this antelope bolo, made in the mosaic inlay style in the 1940s or 1950s. It stands still, looking back as if it hears a sound from behind. Under its feet, there are leaves made of stamped silver work and inlaid turquoise. This is the best antelope figure I have ever seen. Its body is made in the three-dimensional relief technique. It measures 3.26 inches tall and consists of blue/green turquoise, dark brown tortoise shell, and black jet.

Joe Zunie made this antelope bolo in the flush mosaic inlay style in the 1950s or 1960s. Although there is no hallmark on its back, it is, without any doubt, Joe's piece. Its running posture, along with the rock and grass are common among his large games. There are a lot of etchings all over its body. The bolo has larger matching hooves for tips, common in his game bolos. It measures 2.42 inches tall and consists of blue turquoise, orange spiny oyster, gold lip mother of pearl, white mother of pearl, and black jet.

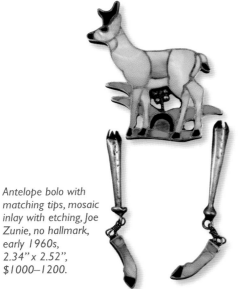

Antelope bolo with matching tips, mosaic inlay with etching, Joe Zunie, no hallmark, early 1960s, 2.34" x 2.52", $1000–1200.

This was made earlier than the bolo just described at left based on the double silver wire clasp on the back. It stands still with a rock and grass under its feet—Joe's signature design. There is no etching on its body. We can see a twisted silver wire and four silver dots amongst its legs, which may signify a yucca flower. The bolo has matching slim legs for tips. It measures 2.52 inches tall and consists of blue/green turquoise, orange spiny oyster, abalone shell, and black jet.

Antelope head pin/pendant, mosaic inlay, Nora Leekity, Nora Leekity, 1970s–80s, 1.94" x 1.58", $200-300.

Nora Leekity made this antelope pin/pendant in the flush mosaic inlay style in the 1970s or 1980s. It measures 1.58 inches tall and consists of blue turquoise, red coral, dark brown pen shell, and black jet.

Antelope pin, mosaic overlay, Juralita Lamy, no hallmark, 1940s–50s, 1.22" x 2.02", $300–450.

In the 1940s or 1950s, Juralita Lamy made this antelope pin in the mosaic overlay style. It is made with green Blue Gem turquoise and black jet. Unstamped silver drops adorn the front of its body and the space between its legs. It looks simple, not naturalistic. It measures 2.02 inches tall.

Antelope tie bar, mosaic overlay, Juralita Lamy, no hallmark, 1940s–50s, 1.04" x 1.88", $300–450.

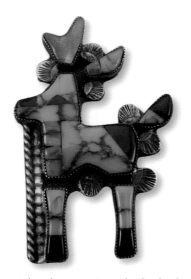

Antelope pin/pendant, mosaic overlay, Juralita Lamy, no hallmark, 1950s–60s, 1.25" x 2.06", $300–450.

Antelope ring, mosaic overlay, Colleen Lamy, C. Lamy, 1970s–80s, 1.14" x 1.97", $160–240.

The same artist also made this antelope tie bar in the same style around the same time. While the antelope just described, above, has a green and black ear, black hip, and green tail, this one has a green and black tail and a green ear. Good artists, Juralita Lamy included, make efforts to bring some variation to different pieces based on a seemingly similar design. In this way, his or her art does not become too repetitive and/or predictable. This antelope measures 1.88 inches tall and consists of green Lone Mountain turquoise and black jet.

Juralita made this antelope pin/pendant, also in the mosaic overlay style, in the 1950s or 1960s. It has a bigger triangular eye than the antelopes described above. It is also more colorful and is adorned with seven stamped silver drops. It has a black hip, a red and green ear, and a black and green upright tail. It measures 2.06 inches tall and consists of green turquoise, red coral, and black jet.

Juralita's daughter Colleen Lamy made this antelope ring in the mosaic overlay style in the 1970s or 1980s. It is confirmed as hers by her nephew, Verden Vacit. It is made in exactly the same design just described, above. However, the stamped silver drops are not in the flower pattern, but in the simple slash pattern. It measures 1.97 inches tall and consists of blue/green turquoise, red spiny oyster, black lip mother of pearl, and black jet.

4

Other Wild Animals

This section includes wild animals rarely made in Zuni jewelry.

Bear bolo with matching tips, mosaic inlay with etching, Joe Zunie, Joe Zuni handwritten, 1960s, 1.79" x 2.63", $1000–1500.

In the 1960s, Joe Zunie made this bear bolo with matching bear paw tips in the flush mosaic inlay style. Although it uses an unstamped Bennett-type clasp, it might have been made in the 1960s because it has a hand-etched hallmark, 'Joe Zuni,' and uses tortoise shell. There are etchings all over its body. We see the familiar rock and grass under its feet, common in his animal pieces. It measures 2.63 inches tall and consists of blue turquoise, red coral, dark brown tortoise shell, and black jet.

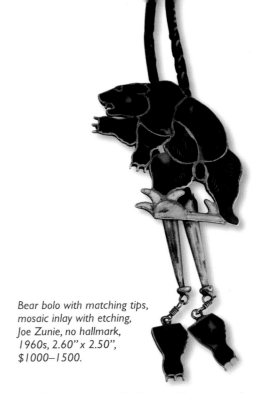

Bear bolo with matching tips, mosaic inlay with etching, Joe Zunie, no hallmark, 1960s, 2.60" x 2.50", $1000–1500.

As there is no hallmark, this was made earlier than the bolo just described at left. The presence of the ground and grass is a variation of his signature. There are etchings all over its body, and it's depicted as trying to intimidate its enemy. It measures 2.5 inches tall and consists of blue turquoise, red coral, and dark brown turtle shell.

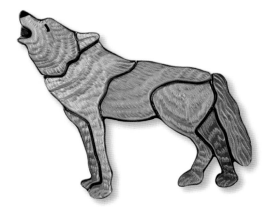

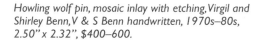

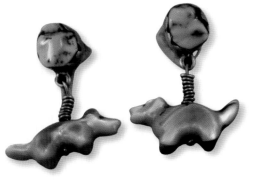

Buffalo bolo with matching tips, mosaic inlay with etching, Jack Mahkee, J. Mahkee handwritten, 1980s, 2.96" x 2.23", $600–900.

Howling wolf pin, mosaic inlay with etching, Virgil and Shirley Benn, V & S Benn handwritten, 1970s–80s, 2.50" x 2.32", $400–600.

Wolf earrings, Carving, Leekya Deyuse, no hallmark, 1940s–50s, 0.94" x 1.14", $1200–1800.

Jack Mahke made this buffalo bolo in the mosaic inlay style in the 1980s. It is not flush inlay. All parts are individually polished and set into channels. The animal stands still in the grassy land, and the front half of its body has some carvings signifying a furry texture. It measures 2.23 inches tall and consists of blue turquoise, light and dark brown pen shell, and black jet.

In the 1970s or 1980s, Virgil and Shirley Ben made this howling wolf pin in the mosaic inlay style. There are numerous carvings all over its body, which give this a realistic texture of fur. This is most certainly a one-of-a-kind piece. It measures 2.32 inches tall and consists of red coral, white mother of pearl, and black jet.

Leekya Deyuse carved these wolf earrings in the 1940s or 1950s. I unknowingly competed against my friend for them in an online auction. After I won the auction, she emailed me that she thought she had been the only one who knew they were made by Leekya Deyuse. Of course, I was very confident that he made them. It measures 1.14 inches tall and is made with red abalone.

Fetish Necklace, Carving, Leekya Deyuse, no hallmark, 1940s–50s, 30", $6000–9000.

The same man made this fetish necklace around the same time. While the majority of the fetishes are birds, there are other animals as well, including coral bears and a red abalone wolf. In addition, there is a green turquoise leaf set far off from the fetishes near the squaw wrap. This fetish necklace was offered to me as compensation, by an online seller, who sold me two small turquoise bear fetishes attributed to Leekya Deyuse, which turned out to be Sarah Leekya's. When I emailed him about it, he provided me with this necklace for a discounted price. The total length of the necklace is thirty inches.

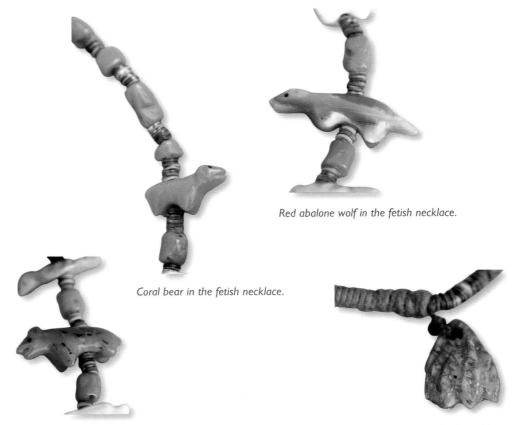

Red abalone wolf in the fetish necklace.

Coral bear in the fetish necklace.

Coral bear in the fetish necklace.

Green turquoise leaf in the fetish necklace.

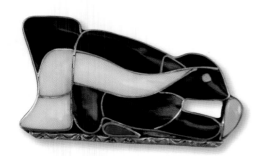

Skunk pin, mosaic inlay, Ann Sheyka, A. Sheyka, 1970s–80s, 1.64" x 0.90", $160–240.

Salmon bolo, mosaic overlay, Nicholas Leekela, no hallmark, 1950s–60s, 2.98" x 2.85", $500–750.

Ann Sheyka made this skunk pin/pendant in the mosaic inlay style in the 1970s or 1980s. It is not made in flush inlay. All pieces are individually formed, polished, and set into channels. This technique gives the piece a three-dimensional effect. It measures 0.90 inches tall and consists of blue turquoise, red coral, white mother of pearl, and black jet.

In the 1950s or 1960s, Nicholas Leekela made this fish bolo in the mosaic overlay style. All fins and tail are made with silver. Even a fin is inlaid in the fish body. It is an extremely rare technique, which I saw, for the first time, in this piece. It measures 2.85 inches tall and consists of blue turquoise, iridescent abalone, white mother of pearl, and silver.

In total, more than twenty wild animals are included in this chapter, and antelopes count most. I would like to comment about the antelopes, deer, and rams made by Joe Zunie and Pauline Dishta Zunie. Some stand still, while others run; some are signed, and others are not. Even if there is no hallmark, their wild animal pieces are identifiably theirs—and marvelous. Some of their bolos have handmade wire clasps, which were used before the introduction of the Bennett-type in 1957. As Joe reportedly began silversmithing in the early 1960s, he may have used the old type of bolo clasp even in the early 1960s.

≡VI≡

Human
Figures

Human Figures have not been made in great quantities in Zuni Jewelry. The *C. G. Wallace Auction Catalogue* includes only four jewelry pieces, excluding human figure carvings made by Leekya and Teddy Weahkee. The famous Hopi maiden pin by Leo Poblano and a standing figure pin by Walter Nakatewa are included in these four.

Zuni man in formal dress bolo with matching tips, mosaic overlay, Della Casi , no hallmark, 1940s–50s, 1.68" x 4.30", $4000–6000.

The artist most likely responsible for this Zuni male figure bolo, made in the mosaic overlay style in the 1940s or 1950s, is Della Casi. It has a W-shape and two round, handmade, silver wire clasps on the back. It has a tubular, silver clasp, for a stand, on the back, as well. This clasp is frequently seen on large pieces made by Leo Poblano and Edward Beyuka, before the introduction of the Bennett-type clasp. An almost identical necklace can be seen in *Southwestern Indian Jewelry* (Cirillo, 1992, p. 215). Its caption says it dates c. 1938, but has no attribution. *Zuni Jewelry* (Bassman, 1992, p. 13) includes four human figure pieces, and the largest female figure pin, in exactly the same style seen in this figure, is attributed to Della Casi. The unique techniques these three pieces have in common are the use of relief carving for facial expression and the use of black pigment. My bolo is a Zuni man in his formal dress. He wears a head scarf, turquoise earrings, a turquoise and coral bead necklace, a concha belt, a bow guard, a bracelet, and moccasin pins. It is extremely well-conceived and well-made. This could just as easily have been made by one of the great artists of the early days of Zuni jewelry. The matching tips greatly enhance the attractiveness of this bolo. It measures 4.30 inches tall and consists of blue turquoise, red pipe stone, white clam shell, white mother of pearl, black jet, silver, and black pigment.

Zuni woman in formal dress earrings, mosaic overlay, Della Casi, no hallmark, 1940s–50s, 0.47" x 1.00", $200–300.

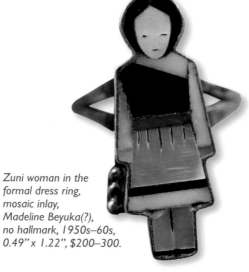

Zuni woman in the formal dress ring, mosaic inlay, Madeline Beyuka(?), no hallmark, 1950s–60s, 0.49" x 1.22", $200–300.

Indian boy bracelet, mosaic inlay, artist unknown, no hallmark, 1950s–60s, central medallion 0.89" x 1.37", $160–240.

In all probability, Della is also the artist who made these Zuni female figure earrings in the mosaic overlay style around the same time. The figures are wearing formal dress. As they are very small, they wear no silver jewelry. They wear manta, apron, and traditional wrap-up shoes, and their eyes and mouths are faintly carved in. They measure 1.00 inch tall and consist of blue turquoise, red spiny oyster, white mother of pearl, and black jet.

Madeline Beyuka is probably the artist responsible for this unmarked Zuni female figure ring, made in the mosaic overlay style in the 1950s or 1960s. I have an identical olla maiden ring apparently made by the same artist. This figure is in her formal dress. She wears manta, apron, and traditional wrap-up shoes. Her eye and mouth are carved in, and black pigment is placed in them. It measures 1.22 inches tall and consists of blue turquoise, red spiny oyster, white mother of pearl, and black jet.

An unknown artist made this Plains Indian boy bracelet in the mosaic overlay style in the 1950s or 1960s. One of my informants attributed it to Madeline Beyuka, but she denied this attribution. It may be souvenir jewelry for tourists. The central figure measures 1.37 inches tall and consists of blue turquoise, red coral, white mother of pearl, and black jet.

Indian boy ring, mosaic inlay, artist unknown, no hallmark, 1950s–60s, 0.84" x 1.12", $80–120.

Apparently, the same artist made this similar Plains Indian boy ring, as well. His eyes and a mouth are inlaid with black jet, just like the bracelet. It measures 1.12 inches tall and consists of blue turquoise, red coral, white mother of pearl, and black jet.

Hopi maiden necklace, mosaic inlay, Emma Bonney(?), no hallmark, 1950s–60s, 1.35" x 3.04", $300–450.

A Navajo artist named Emma Bonney is probably responsible for this Hopi Maiden necklace, made in the mosaic inlay style in the 1950s or 1960s. A nearly identical pin is featured in *Southwest Silver Jewelry* (Baxter. 2001, p. 164). Its caption attributes it as "Zuni or Hopi." Her eyes, eye brows, nose, and mouth are simply etched—it looks like a layman's work. It measures 3.04 inches tall and consists of blue turquoise, red coral, white mother of pearl and black jet.

Indian maiden pin/pendant, mosaic inlay, Virgil and Shirley Benn, Virgil & Shirley Benn, 1990s, 1.88" x 3.03", $400–600.

Virgil and Shirley Benn made this Plains Indian girl pin/pendant in the mosaic inlay style in the 1990s. Her hair is expertly carved to show the texture of her beautiful black locks. She wears a hair ornament with a feather, hanging from the top of her head, and a necklace with a red centerpiece. It measures 3.03 inches tall and consists of blue turquoise, red spiny oyster, gold lip mother of pearl, purple lip oyster shell, white mother of pearl, and black jet.

I have collected less than ten human figures, excluding olla maidens, included in my third book. Among these ten pieces, the Zuni man in the formal dress bolo with matching tips is the best. I have seen its female version, made by the same artist, in an online auction, which I failed to acquire. If I had succeeded, this chapter would have been greatly improved.

≡ VII ≡

Flowers, Leaves, and Foliates

The *C. G. Wallace Auction Catalogue* includes thirty-six flower, leaf, and foliate pieces. Eight of them were made in the 1930s.

Flower pin, channel inlay, artist unknown, no hallmark, 1950s–60s, 1.12" x 1.58", $180–240.

Flower head bolo, channel inlay, Lambert Homer Sr., no hallmark, 1930s–40s, 2.16" across, $1000–1500.

An unknown artist made this flower pin in the channel inlay style in the 1950s or 1960s. While we may see a lot of flower head designs by various artists, this flower design, with leaves and stem, is very rare. This design is not of a specific species, but of a generic flower. Although its stem and leaves are quite large, combined with its flower head, it is extremely pretty. It measures 1.58 inches tall and consists of Blue Gem turquoise, red coral, and white mother of pearl.

In the 1930s or 1940s, Lambert Homer Sr. made this flower bolo in the channel inlay style. It is very similar to the famous concha belt made by Lambert Homer Sr. and Roger Skeet, in 1936. As it is smaller, its flower design may have become simpler as a result. The silver work of this bolo might have been done by Roger Skeet, as well. One of my informants attributed it to Della Casi, though. The turquoise used is Blue Gem Mine. It measures 2.16 inches in diameter.

Foliate earrings, channel inlay, Della Casi(?), no hallmark, 1940s–60s, 0.94" x 0.97", $200–300.

Della Casi probably made these foliate earrings, done in channel inlay in the 1940s or 1960s. This set is similar to the first two sets of earrings made by Alice Leekya Homer in this section. However, it is different in that the three leaves come from the side of the circle, while three similar leaves come from the top of the circle in Leekya's sets. They measure 0.97 inches tall and consists of Blue Gem turquoise.

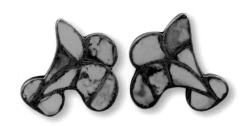

Flower earrings, channel inlay, Myra Tucson, no hallmark, 1940s–50s, 1.03" x 1.03", $180–240.

Myra Tucson made these flower earrings in the channel inlay style in the 1940s or 1950s. Although all the parts are made of blue/green turquoise, they are clearly flowers. They measure 1.03 inches tall and consist of Blue Gem turquoise.

Flower earrings, channel inlay, Alice Leekya Homer, no hallmark, 1950s–60s, 0.70" x 0.67", $120–180.

These flower earrings were made by Alice Leekya Homer in the channel inlay style in the 1950s or 1960s. They have screw-in clasps on their backs. They measure 0.67 inches tall.

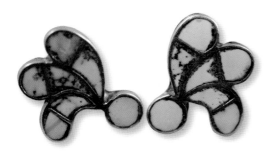

Flower earrings, channel inlay, Alice Leekya Homer, no hallmark, 1950s–60s, 0.78" x 0.86", $120–180.

These earrings by Alice Leekya Homer, made in the channel inlay style in the 1950s or 1960s, are virtually identical to the previous pair. One of my informants attributed them to Annie Quam Gasper. They have screw-in clasps on their backs, and they measure 0.86 inches tall.

Flower Earrings, channel inlay, Alice Leekya Homer, no hallmark, 1950s–60s, 0.42" x 0.72", $80–120.

Alice Leekya Homer made these flower earrings, as well, in the channel inlay style in the 1950s or 1960s. They have screw-in clasps on their backs, and they measure 0.72 inches tall.

Yucca pin, channel inlay, Annie Quam Gasper, no hallmark, 1950s–60s, 1.60" x 1.56", $300–450.

This yucca pin in mosaic inlay was made by Annie Quam Gasper in the 1950s or 1960s. As opposed to the three previous sets of earrings, made by Alice Leekya Homer in the flush inlay technique, this pin is carved three-dimensionally, and then set. It measures 1.56 inches tall and consists of Blue Gem turquoise.

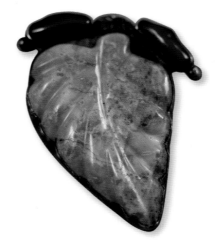

Leaf ring, carving, Leekya Deyuse, silver work by Dan Simplicio, no hallmark, 1940s–50s, 1.46" x 2.09", $1600–2400.

Leaf pin, carving, Leekya Deyuse, silver work by Dan Simplicio, no hallmark, 1940s–50s, 1.86" x 2.28", $1800–2700.

Yucca Earrings, channel inlay, Annie Quam Gasper, no hallmark, 1950s–60s, 0.56" x 0.83", $120–180.

Annie Quam Gasper also made these matching yucca earrings in the mosaic inlay style in the 1950s or 1960s. They measure 0.83 inches tall.

This leaf pin was carved by Leekya Deyuse and set on silver backing by Dan Simplicio Sr. in the 1940s or 1950s. It was converted from a bolo, and has an oblong stamped silver drop between two coral twigs, which can be considered a hallmark of Dan's. It measures 2.28 inches tall and consists of turquoise and ox-blood coral.

Leekya Deyuse and Dan Simplicio Sr. worked together on this leaf pin, as well, around the same time. These attributions were confirmed by one of Leekya Deyuse's granddaughters and Dan Simplicio Jr. Apparently, based on the marks on its back, it originally had a Keystone-shaped bolo clasp, and was later converted to a pin. The coral parts were oriented on the bottom when it was a bolo, but everything was set upside down when it was converted to a pin. It measures 2.09 inches tall and consists of turquoise and ox-blood coral.

Leaf ring, carving, Leekya Deyuse, silver work by Leonard Martza, no hallmark, 1950s–60s, 0.41" x 0.81", $500–750.

Leaf ring, carving, Ben Eustace, no hallmark, 1950s–60s, 0.74" x 1.22", $160–240.

Leaf ring, carving, Sally Poblano, S. Poblano, 1970s–80s, 0.61" x 0.87", $120–180.

In the 1950s or 1960s, Leekya Deyuse carved this leaf ring and Leonard Martza set it on silver backing. One of Leekya Deyuse's granddaughters told me she had seen a similar ring that exhibited Leekya and Leonard's joint works. The carved leaves are similar to the one on my Leekya fetish necklace, and to the following leaves made by Ben Eustace. It measures 0.81 inches tall.

Ben Eustace made this turquoise leaf ring in the 1950s or 1960s. The combination of turquoise leaf carvings and this kind of silver leaf is his original design. It measures 1.22 inches tall.

This leaf ring was made by Sally Poblano in the 1970s or 1980s. The turquoise and coral leaves are set with the Simplicio-style silver leaf. It measures 0.87 inches tall.

Leaf pendant, carving, Doris Ondelacy, silver work by Lorraine Waatsa, no hallmark, 1960s, 2.15" x 2.87", $1200–1800.

Doris Ondelacy carved this leaf pendant in the 1960s, and her granddaughter, Lorraine Waatsa, set it in July, 2012. Lorraine inherited it through her mother, Alice Quam. She showed me the carving and asked if I wanted it. I answered, "Yes, of course," at once. Then, she set it into the silver frame. It measures 2.87 inches tall and is made with a Lone Mountain turquoise.

The reverse side of the leaf pendant.

Fifteen plants are included in this chapter. The carved turquoise leaves are especially marvelous. While those made by Leekya Deyuse and Dan Simplicio are particularly fascinating, the Ondelacy piece is invaluable, as well. It should be noted that Doris and Warren Ondelacy also worked in nugget work style, shown in their butterfly piece in chapter two.

≡ VIII ≡

Cultural Objects
and
Symbols

The *C. G. Wallace Auction Catalogue* includes cultural objects and symbols such as crosses, arrows, wagons, and Shriners' symbols. These and others are included in my collection, as well.

1 Crosses

Twelve crosses are included in the C. G. Wallace Collection Catalogue. Their years of make are fully recorded: three from the 1920s, seven from the 1930s, and two from the 1940s. Juan de Dios made four, Annie Quam Gasper and Dan Simplicio made two pieces each, and Della Casi, Tom Paquin, Rosalie Jamon, and Ella Quam made one piece each. It is very interesting that the famous Iule cross is not included.

Cross pendant, cast and channel inlay, Juan de Dios(?), no hallmark, 1930s-40s, 1.14" x 2.18", $400–600.

This cross pendant, made in the cast and channel inlay styles in the 1930s or 1940s, is probably Juan de Dios's work. Although one of my informants attributed it to Horace Iule, based on the cast work and rough-looking stone work, I have chosen to attribute it to Juan. As Juan was active till the beginning of the 1940s, it is impossible to find an informant who knows Juan's pieces well in Zuni. This kind of rough turquoise inlay work might be characteristic of his style. Please refer to his Knifewing (Sei, 2010, p. 47). This cross measures 2.18 inches tall.

Cross pendant, cast and channel inlay, Juan de Dios, no hallmark, 1930s–40s, 1.49" x 2.42", $400–600.

Juan de Dios most likely made this cross pendant, which is in the cast and channel inlay styles, around the same time. This turquoise setting is lower and smoother than the one just described, above. The stamp patterns on this cross are slightly different, too. However, the basic designs and constructions of both are essentially identical. It measures 2.42 inches tall and consists of seven Lone Mountain turquoise cabochons.

Cross pendant, cast and nugget work, Horace Iule, H. Iule, 1970s, 2.13" x 2.72", $400–600.

This cross pendant was made by Horace Iule in the cast and nugget work styles in the 1970s. It is the typical Iule cross for which he has long been known. The stamps on the cross are characteristic of his technique. It measures 2.72 inches tall and consists of seven Sleeping Beauty turquoise cabochons.

Cross pendant, cast and nugget work, Horace Iule, H. Iule, 1970s, 1.92" x 2.72", $400–600.

Around the same time, Horace Iule also made this cross pendant in the cast and nugget work styles. Each end of the cross is rectangular, and three of them are stamped with a flower-like die. It measures 2.72 inches tall and consists of eight seemingly Kingman turquoise cabochons.

Cross pendant, cast and nugget work, Horace Iule, H. Iule, 1970s, 2.01" x 2.79", $400–600.

Here is another cross pendant by Horace Iule. It was made in the cast and nugget work styles in the 1970s. Three ends of the cross are round, and the remaining one is rectangular. These three round ends are stamped with the same flower-like die used on the cross just described, above. It measures 2.79 inches tall and consists of eight Kingman turquoise cabochons.

Cross pendant, snake eye, Myra Tsipa Qualo, Myra Qualo, 1970s–80s, 1.73" x 2.12", $200–300.

In the 1970s or 1980s, Myra Tsipa Qualo made this cross pendant in the snake eye style. Her daughter, June Qualo, makes cross designs that are similar to Myra's. However, there is a difference: Myra sets eight silver wires for the adornment of her cross, and three flower stamps on each end, while June sets four silver wires, and no stamp (Levy, 1980, p. 58). It measures 2.12 inches tall.

Cross pendant, mosaic inlay, Artist unknown, no hallmark, 1950s–60s, 1.13" x 1.48", $100–150.

This is a cross pendant made by an unknown artist in the mosaic inlay style in the 1950s or 1960s. One of my informants attributed it to Lena Paywa Theslakia, but she denied it was hers. It is a small and cute piece. It measures 1.48 inches tall, including the bail, and consists of blue turquoise, red coral, white mother of pearl, and black jet.

Cross pendant, cast and channel inlay, artist unknown, no hallmark, 1950s–60s, 2.20" x 2.93", $200–300.

In the 1950s or 1960s, a Navajo silversmith named Yazzie cast this well-designed cross pendant, which was then inlaid skillfully by an unknown Zuni lapidary. We may occasionally see crosses in the same design, but with a chip inlay. It measures 2.93 inches tall and consists of blue/green turquoise, red coral, and white clam shell.

2 Arrows, Arrow Heads, and Spear Heads

The C. G. Wallace Auction Catalogue includes seven arrow and arrow head pieces. One piece each was made by Juan de Dios, Winnie Jamon, John Lucio, and Jerry Watson. The remaining three pieces were made by unknown artists.

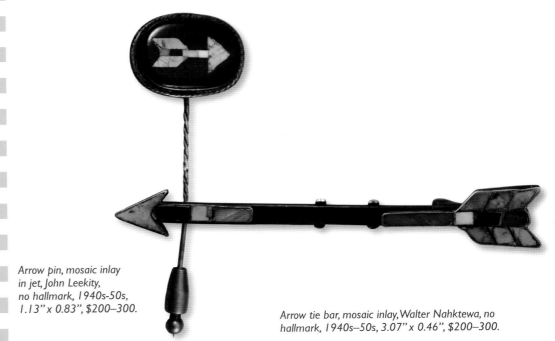

Arrow pin, mosaic inlay in jet, John Leekity, no hallmark, 1940s-50s, 1.13" x 0.83", $200–300.

Arrow tie bar, mosaic inlay, Walter Nahktewa, no hallmark, 1940s–50s, 3.07" x 0.46", $200–300.

John Leekity (Gordon Leak) made this arrow stick pin in the mosaic inlay in jet style in the 1940s or 1950s. The silver pin is partly twisted, bent near its end at a right angle, and its end is welded onto the backing of the inlaid arrow. It measures 0.83 inches tall and consists of blue/green turquoise, orange spiny oyster, white mother of pearl, and black jet.

This arrow tie bar was made by Walter Nahktewa in the mosaic inlay style in the 1940s or 1950s. Separated in the middle by a length of 0.94 inches, it is for an extremely wide necktie. It measures 3.07 inches wide and consists of blue/green turquoise, orange spiny oyster, white mother of pearl, and black jet.

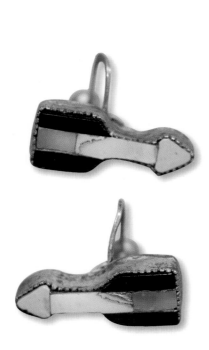

Arrow earrings, mosaic overlay, Della Casi, no hallmark, 1940s–50s, 0.83" x 0.36", $200–300.

In the 1940s or 1950s, Della Casi made these arrow earrings in the mosaic overlay style. They are cute, tiny pieces, measuring 0.36 inches tall, and consist of blue/green turquoise, orange spiny oyster, white mother of pearl, and black jet.

Arrow head bolo, channel inlay, Della Casi, no hallmark, 1940s–50s, 1.36" x 1.85", $1000–1500.

Della Casi made this arrow head Bolo tie in the 1940s or 1950s in the channel inlay style. Its silver backing is a bit concave, and two heavily stamped silver platelets are welded on both sides. A rough-surfaced turquoise piece is set in each channel. This kind of channel inlay is similar to the one used by Juan de Dios. It measures 1.85 inches tall and consists of Blue Gem turquoise.

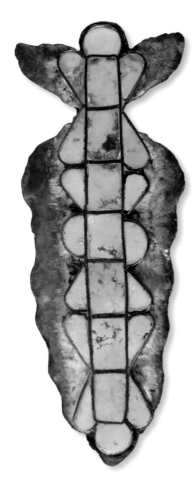

This spear head bolo, or scarf slide, was made in the 1940s or 1950s by Nora Leekity's husband, William Leekity, in the channel inlay style. It has a single platelet for a clasp, and measures 2.69 inches tall, consisting of Blue Gem turquoise.

Mary Ann Cellicion, Dexter Cellicion's second wife, made these arrow earrings in the 1950s or 1960s in the mosaic inlay in jet style. Three inlaid dots in each earring enhance their beauty. Almost all pieces in this style have been attributed to John Leekity, but some should be attributed to Mary Ann. It measures 0.74 inches tall and consists of blue turquoise, orange spiny oyster, white mother of pearl, and black jet.

The only wagon motif featured in the C. G. Wallace Auction Catalogue was made by Frank Dishta.

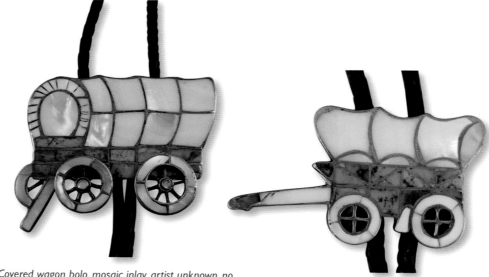

Covered wagon bolo, mosaic inlay, artist unknown, no hallmark, 1940s–50s, 2.73" x 2.18", $600–900.

Covered wagon pin, channel inlay, unknown artist, no hallmark, 1940s–1950s, 2.36" x 1.33", $600–900.

In the 1940s or 1950s, an unknown artist made this covered wagon bolo in the mosaic inlay style. Its two freely turning, inlaid wheels are rarely seen in Zuni jewelry. One of my informants attributed it to Joe Zunie, but I am too suspicious of this claim to give Joe Zunie the credit. It measures 2.18 inches tall and consists of blue/green turquoise and white mother of pearl. The use of only two colors is rare, as well.

This covered wagon bolo was made by an unknown artist in the 1940s or 1950s in the mosaic inlay style. This and the first wagon both consist of only two colors—blue turquoise and white mother of pearl—but the cover of this wagon looks more naturalistic. Also distinguishing this design is a break near the rear wheel. It measures 1.33 inches tall.

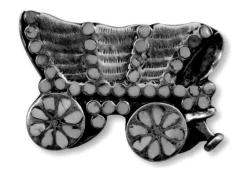

Covered wagon pin, channel inlay, Virgil Dishta Sr., no hallmark, 1940s–60s, 1.38" x 0.97", $600–900.

Sometime between the 1940s and 1960s, Virgil Dishta Sr. made this covered wagon pin in the Dishta style channel inlay. Blue turquoise bits were shaped, inlaid, polished flat, and placed into holes dug out in all parts of the wagon, including wheels, brake, and cover, each of which was made separately and welded onto the silver base. It measures 0.97 inches tall.

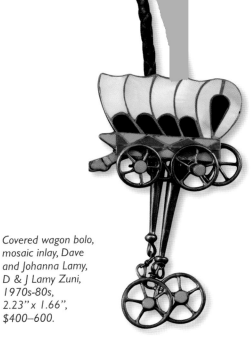

Covered wagon bolo, mosaic inlay, Dave and Johanna Lamy, D & J Lamy Zuni, 1970s-80s, 2.23" x 1.66", $400–600.

This is a covered wagon bolo made by Dave and Johanna Lamy in the mosaic inlay style in the 1970s or 1980s. A similar covered wagon bolo, under the name(s) "D. J. Lamy," is featured in *Jewelry by Southwest American Indians: Evolving Designs* (Schiffer, 1990, p. 101). Its two wheels can turn, and similar wheels are used as tips. It measures 1.66 inches tall and consists of blue turquoise, red coral, white mother of pearl, and black jet.

Covered wagon bolo, mosaic inlay, Juralita Lamy, no hallmark, 1980s, 2.17" x 1.65", $400–600.

In the 1980s, Juralita Lamy made this covered wagon bolo in the mosaic inlay style. Although there is no hallmark, it is confirmed as hers by a sister of Lamy's son-in-law. It is almost identical to the one just described, above, except for red and green painting on the sideboard and the reversed colors. As for the sideboard's design, it is exactly the same as the one in Schiffer's book. It measures 1.65 inches tall and consists of blue/green turquoise, red coral, white mother of pearl and, black jet.

Covered wagon bolo, mosaic inlay, Joe Zunie, Joe Zunie JZJ, 1960s–80s, 2.58" x 2.33", $600–900.

Covered wagon bolo, mosaic inlay, Joe Zunie, no hallmark, 1950s–60s, 3.03" x 1.99", $600–900.

Covered wagon bolo, mosaic inlay, Lincoln Zunie, H-L Zunie, 2010, 2.57" x 2.01", $400–600.

Joe Zunie made this covered wagon bolo in the mosaic inlay style in the 1960s or 1970s. It has larger, matching wheels for tips on the side of the wagon. It measures 2.33 inches tall and consists of blue/green turquoise, red coral, white mother of pearl, and dark brown tortoise shell.

This covered wagon bolo was also made by Joe Zunie in the mosaic inlay style around the same time. Although there is no hallmark, it is apparently Joe's work. It has a painted pattern on the sideboard identical to the one on Dave and Johanna Lamy's wagon. It measures 1.99 inches tall and consists of blue/green turquoise, red coral, white mother of pearl, and black jet.

Lincoln Zunie made this covered wagon bolo in 2010 in the mosaic inlay style. When I visited Raylan and Patsy Zunie Edaakie, and asked about her uncle Lincoln, she took me to his house. I talked with Lincoln for a little while, and, just before I left, he provided me with this bolo. His sideboard pattern is different from those made by other artists. Moreover, all wheels, including tips, are inlaid with turquoise and coral. It measures 2.01 inches tall and consists of blue turquoise, red coral, and white mother of pearl.

4 Shriners' Symbols

There are two pieces in the C. G. Wallace Auction Catalogue with the caption, "sword, crescent and star," which might represent the Shriners' symbol. The Shriners are a fraternity that was founded in 1872, in New York. They have built and currently operate 22 hospitals in the United States, one in Canada, and another in Mexico.*

*For more information on the Shriners and their children's hospitals, visit http://www.beashrinernow.com/en.aspx.

Shriners' symbol bolo, mosaic inlay in spiny oyster, Bruce Zunie, no hallmark, 1950s–60s, 2.17" x 2.24", $1000–1500.

In the 1950s or 1960s, Bruce Zunie made this Shriners' symbol bolo in the mosaic inlay in spiny oyster shell style. An informant mentioned the name of Merle Edaakie, however, as the artist responsible. The oyster shell is backed with a silver plate, with two triangular silver pieces added to the bottom. As a result, it looks like a scallop shell. A sword, crescent, and five-point star are carved, separately, in the shell. It measures 2.24 inches tall and consists of green turquoise, orange spiny oyster, black jet, and silver.

Shriners' symbol bolo, mosaic inlay, artist unknown, no hallmark, 1950s, 2.17" x 2.24", $600–900.

Shriners' symbol bolo, mosaic inlay, John Lucio, no hallmark, 1950s, 2.17" x 2.24", $600–900.

Shriners' symbol bolo, channel inlay, Bruce Zunie, no hallmark, 1940s–50s, 1.96" x 1.57", $600–900.

An unknown artist made this Shriners' symbol bolo in the mosaic inlay style in the 1950s. It accompanies a third place ribbon, awarded at the New Mexico State Fair, held in 1959. A carved human head representing the Egyptian sphinx is inlaid in the top center portion of the crescent. A sword is inserted into the crescent moon from its back left to the front right. From the center of the sword, a five-point star hangs down. It measures 2.24 inches tall and consists of blue/green turquoise, red coral, fossilized ivory, white mother of pearl, and black jet.

In the 1950s, John Lucio made this Shriners' symbol bolo in the mosaic inlay style. The construction of this bolo is identical to the one just described, above. The carved face resembles the one in his Comanche Dancer design, which is sometimes attributed to Teddy Weahkee. It measures 2.24 inches tall and consists of blue/green turquoise, red spiny oyster, white mother of pearl, and black jet.

Bruce Zunie made this Shriners' symbol bolo in the channel inlay style in the 1940s or 1950s. A sword is set above the crescent moon, inside of which a five-point star is attached. This configuration resembles the first Shriners' bolo in the chapter attributed to Bruce Zunie, made in the spiny oyster shell style. It measures 1.57 inches tall and consists of blue/green turquoise and silver.

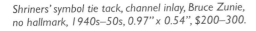

Shriners' symbol tie tack, channel inlay, Bruce Zunie, no hallmark, 1940s–50s, 0.97" x 0.54", $200–300.

Around the same time, Bruce Zunie made this Shriners' symbol tie tack in the channel inlay style. I acquired it as a set with the bolo just described, above. The placement of the three main figures is different from Bruce's bolos, but consistent with the standard Shriners' emblem design. It measures 0.54 inches tall and consists of blue/green turquoise and silver.

Shriners' symbol bolo, mosaic inlay, Tony and Rita Edaakie, no hallmark, 1940s–1950s, 2.07" x 1.24", $400–600.

Tony and Rita Edaakie made this Shriners' symbol bolo in the mosaic inlay style in the 1940s or 1950s. This follows the standard design: a colorful crescent moon with a sword inserted from the back left to the front right, and a five-point star hanging from the center of the sword. It measures 1.24 inches tall and consists of blue/green turquoise, red abalone, white mother of pearl, black jet, and silver.

Shriners' symbol bolo, mosaic inlay, Tony and Rita Edaakie, no hallmark, 1940s–50s, 2.38" x 1.26", $400–600.

Within the same time period, Tony and Rita Edaakie made this Shriners' symbol bolo as well, in the mosaic inlay style. Unlike the previously described bolo, this has silver walls set inside the crescent moon. It measures 1.26 inches tall and consists of green turquoise, red coral, orange spiny oyster, white mother of pearl, black jet, and silver.

5 Other Cultural Objects or Symbols

This category is devoted to miscellaneous subjects, such as pots, fan and gourd, initials, and geometric designs.

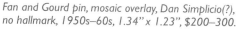

Fan and Gourd pin, mosaic overlay, Dan Simplicio(?), no hallmark, 1950s–60s, 1.34" x 1.23", $200–300.

This is a fan and gourd pin, probably made by Dan Simplicio in the 1950s or 1960s, in the mosaic overlay style. It is a very rare motif; besides this, I have seen only two fan and gourd pieces. Two chains hang from the ends of the handles. It measures 1.23 inches tall and consists of green turquoise, red coral, dark brown tortoise shell, white mother of pearl, black jet, and yellow shell.

Pottery jar earrings, mosaic overlay, Teddy Weahkee(?), no hallmark, 1950s–60s, 0.69" x 0.71", $200–300.

These olla earrings, made in the mosaic overlay style in the 1940s or 1950s, can most likely be attributed to Teddy Weahkee, according to one of my trader friends. They are classical and cute, measure 0.71 inches tall, and consist of green turquoise, orange spiny oyster, white mother of pearl, and black jet.

Flaming pottery jar earrings, mosaic overlay, Madeline Beyuka(?), no hallmark, 1950s–60s, 0.71" x 1.12, $160–240.

Initial bolo, mosaic inlay, David Tsikewa, David, 1940s–50s, 1.45" x 1.81", $600–900.

Abstract bolo, mosaic inlay in clam shell, Merle Edaakie, no hallmark, 1940s–50s, 2.82" x 1.95", $2000–3000.

Madeline Beyuka is probably the artist responsible for these flaming pot earrings made in the mosaic inlay style in the 1950s or 1960s. I thought they were ollas for use in a fireplace in an ancient Zuni house, while a Zuni artist I know described them as outdoor mutton stew pots. Either way, they are extremely rare in Zuni jewelry. They measure 1.12 inches tall and consist of blue/green turquoise, red coral, white mother of pearl, and black jet.

In the 1940s or 1950s, David Tsikewa made this Initial bolo in the mosaic inlay style. It has his hallmark, "DAVID." A smaller capital L sits inside a larger O. It is a fine example of the bolos and buckles, described in *Zuni Fetish Carvers: The Mid-Century Masters* (McManis, 2003, p.21), that bear customers' initials. It measures 1.81 inches tall and consists of light green turquoise and red coral.

In the 1940s or 1950s, Merle Edaakie made this geometric design bolo in the mosaic inlay in clam shell style. I have no idea what particular design it is supposed to stand for. There are a lot of geometric design pieces in the *C. G. Wallace Collection Catalogue*—this might be one of them. It is a very rare and superb piece for sure. It measures 1.95 inches tall and consists of blue/green turquoise, orange spiny oyster, white mother of pearl, and black jet.

Geometric bolo, silver overlay and mosaic inlay, artist unknown, no hallmark, 1.49" x 1.83", 1950s–60s, $600-900.

Geometric bolo, mosaic inlay, artist unknown, no hallmark, 1940s–50s, 1.08" x 2.15", $300–450.

Geometric bolo, silver overlay and mosaic inlay, Dennis Edaakie, no hallmark, 1950s–60s, 1.44" x 2.26", $1000–1500.

Dennis Edaakie made this geometric bolo in the silver overlay/mosaic inlay style in the 1950s or 1960s. It might be a variation of the Rain Bird design frequently seen on the older Zuni pottery. It measures 2.26 inches tall and consists of blue turquoise, red coral, dark brown tortoise shell, white mother of pearl, and black jet.

This is a geometric bolo made by an unknown artist in the silver overlay/mosaic inlay style in the 1950s or 1960s. It might be a parrot design, for it has an eye, a large beak, and tail feathers. One of my informants attributed it to Quincy Peynetsa. A well-conceived and well-executed piece, it measures 1.83 inches tall and consists of blue turquoise, red coral, orange spiny oyster, white mother of pearl, and black jet.

An unknown artist made this geometric bolo in the silver overlay/mosaic inlay style in the 1940s or 1950s. Its shape reminds me of a neck tie. One of my informants has attributed it to Andrew Dewa. I am skeptical about this claim, but it is a cute and pretty piece. It measures 2.15 inches tall and consists of blue/green turquoise, red coral, orange spiny oyster, white mother of pearl, and black jet.

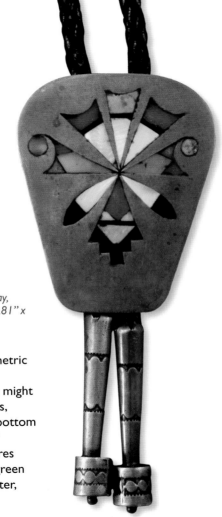

Geometric bolo, silver overlay and mosaic inlay, Quincy Peynetsa, no hallmark, 1950s–60s, 1.81" x 2.24", $200–300.

Quincy Peynetsa made this geometric bolo in the 1950s-1960s in the silver overlay/mosaic inlay style. This design might represent a collection of bird feathers, probably of an eagle. The one in the bottom center reminds me of a headdress of Knifewing or Rainbow Man. It measures 2.24 inches tall and consists of blue/green turquoise, red coral, yellow spiny oyster, white mother of pearl, and black jet.

Just under forty pieces are included in this chapter. Among crosses, two pieces attributed to Juan de Dios are marvelous. His turquoise inlay technique is unique.

As for arrows, we should be very careful about attribution. The pieces made by John Leekity (Gordon Leak) and Mary Ann Cellicion, for example, are very similar.

Juralita Lamy, Joe and Pauline Dishta Zunie, and Helen and Lincoln Zunie are famous for their covered wagon designs. However, they might have forerunner: two blue-and-white covered wagons, made by unknown artists, and another made by Virgil Dishta Sr., might have come first.

Lastly, I have to call attention to the newer motif: the Shriners' symbol. This motif might have appeared just after the World War II. Even though the motif itself is a newcomer in terms of Zuni jewelry history, the designs and executions based on them are completely authentic.

Rain Bird
and
Hummingbird

These two Jewelry designs were borrowed from the older Zuni pottery designs representing the clouds bringing severe thunder storms to Zuni Land. The Zunis are eager to pray to Kachinas for rain all year round in the form of religious dancing, and rain is believed to be a visit from their ancestors to the village.

1 *Rain Birds*

Two of the greatest artists in Zuni jewelry history worked with this design: Dan Simplicio and Frank Vacit, both of whom worked for the C. G. Wallace Trading Post.

The C. G. Wallace Auction Catalogue features two Rain Bird pieces, one by Dan Simplicio, in 1945 (#100), and the other by Lambert Homer Jr., in 1954 (#933). Southwester Silver Jewelry features a Rain Bird ring made by Frank Vacit in the 1940s (Baxter, 2001, p. 142), which is in the older C. G. Wallace collection. Meanwhile, the C. G. Wallace Collection housed in the Heard Museum includes a bracelet with a more complicated Rain Bird design (Slaney, 1998, p. 30).

It can be very difficult to confirm who made individual Rain Bird pieces. Neither Dan Simplicio Jr. nor Bessie Vacit can provide me with a solid solution. Consequently, the following attributions are based on my best guesses.

Rain Bird bolo, silver overlay and mosaic inlay, Dan Simplicio(?), no hallmark, 1940s–50s, 1.52" x 1.81", $1600–2400.

Dan Simplicio probably made this Rain Bird bolo, done in the silver overlay/mosaic inlay style in the 1940s or 1950s. As there is no apparent border in its edges, I judge it is Dan's. The center space, which is encircled by three feathers, looks round. It measures 1.81 inches tall and consists of blue/green turquoise, red abalone shell, white mother of pearl, and black jet.

Rain Bird necklace, silver overlay and mosaic inlay, Frank Vacit(?), no hallmark, 1960s–70s, central medallion 1.72" x 1.40", $800–1200.

Rain Bird pin, silver overlay and mosaic inlay, Frank Vacit(?), no hallmark, 1940s–60s, 1.51" x 2.05", $800–1200.

Sometime between the 1940s and 1960s, Frank Vacit probably most likely made this Rain Bird pin in the silver overlay/ mosaic inlay style. Stamped borders run along the upper and bottom edges. It's characteristic of Frank's style. The bird design is bolder than the previous one. It measures 2.05 inches tall and consists of blue/green turquoise, red coral, white mother of pearl, and black jet.

It's very likely that it was Frank Vacit who made this Rain Bird necklace in the silver overlay/mosaic inlay style in the 1960s or 1970s. It has stamps on the back that read "hand made" and "sterling." The Rain Bird design of the central medallion is framed by black borders, while the two smaller side pieces are not. A black circle, or point, lies in the center of both side pieces, but there appears to be an empty circle, constructed with three Rain Bird beaks, in the center of the large medallion. The central medallion measures 1.40 inches tall and consists of blue/green turquoise, red coral, white mother of pearl, and black jet.

Rain bird bracelet, silver overlay and mosaic inlay, Frank Vacit(?), no hallmark, 1960s–70s, 1.39" x 1.71", $800–1200.

This is a matching Rain Bird bracelet, also made, most likely, by Frank Vacit. The medallion, like the central piece in the previous example, has borders inlaid with black jet. It measures 1.71 inches tall.

Rain bird bolo, mosaic inlay in tortoise shell, Dan Simplicio(?), no hallmark, 1950s-60s, 2.07" x 2.60", $1200–1800.

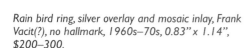

Rain bird ring, silver overlay and mosaic inlay, Frank Vacit(?), no hallmark, 1960s–70s, 0.83" x 1.14", $200–300.

Rain bird earrings, silver overlay and mosaic inlay, Frank Vacit(?), no hallmark, 1960s–70s, 0.76" x 1.16", $200–300.

The same artist is attributed to this matching Rain Bird ring. There is a black circle in the center of the ring face, which is identical to the one seen in the side pieces of the necklace. It measures 1.14 inches tall.

These matching Rain Bird earrings, made in the same design as the preceding ring just described, are also attributed to Frank Vacit. They have screw-in clasps on their backs, and measure 1.16 inches tall.

This Rain Bird bolo was probably made by Dan Simplicio, done in the 1950s or 1960s, in the mosaic inlay in tortoise shell style. Unlike the following two pieces, there is no small circle in the center. Its silver work does not look Zuni to me. It measures 2.60 inches tall and consists of blue/green turquoise, red coral, dark brown tortoise shell, white mother of pearl, and black jet.

Rain Bird bolo, mosaic inlay in tortoise shell, Dan Simplicio, no hallmark, 1950s-60s, 1.45" x 1.81", $1000–1500.

Rain bird bracelet, mosaic inlay in tortoise shell, Dan Simplicio(?), no hallmark, central medallion 1.26" x 1.50", 1950s–60s, $1200–1800.

The same artist made this Rain Bird bolo in the mosaic inlay in the tortoise shell style in the 1950s or 1960s. It has a small center circle made of green turquoise. Except for this point, its lapidary work is the same as the previous bolo, and its silver work doesn't look Zuni either, even if it is smaller. It measures 1.81 inches tall and consists of blue/green turquoise, red coral, dark brown tortoise shell, white mother of pearl, and black jet.

Dan Simplicio probably made this Rain Bird bracelet, in the mosaic inlay in tortoise shell style in the 1950s or 1960s, as well. Its Rain Bird design is almost identical to the one just described, and the silver work here does not look Zuni either. The four overhanging silver parts that prevent the insert from popping are characteristic of Dan's work. The insert measures 1.20 inches tall and consists of blue/green turquoise, red coral, dark brown tortoise shell, white mother of pearl, and black jet.

Drawing of the differences in hummingbird designs by Ellen Quandelacy and Annie Quam Gasper.

Annie Quam Gasper, Ellen Quandelacy's sister and next-door neighbor, originated this design. According to Slaney:

> Two of the most well-known channel designs, the "hummingbird" and the "spiderweb" patterns were invented by Gasper and are still used by the Quam and Quandelacy families today. The idea for the spiral-shaped hummingbird design, called the butterfly or whirlwind design by Dale S. King, was inspired by the pottery designs of her uncle, Milone.... Both patterns incorporate negative space into the designs; an open "S" shape is an integral part of the hummingbird design, and an open circle "D" is often present in the spiderweb design. The open areas break up the surfaces and contribute to the lightness of the pieces. (1998. p. 40)

Both Annie and Ellen used the Hummingbird design prolifically in their jewelry. It can be very difficult to say what is Annie's and what is Ellen's.

Two years ago, one of Ellen's daughters, Faye Quandelacy, drew me a picture, which is consistent with designs seen in other books on Zuni jewelry, that illustrates the difference between the Hummingbird designs of Ellen and Annie, examples of which can be found in *Zuni: The Art and the People II* (Bell, 1975, p. 44) and *III* (Bell, 1976, p. 53), respectively. In addition, we can see in the photos in this book Ellen's similar hummingbird design without space in the center. However, the drawing of Annie's design does not correspond with the Hummingbird set she made that is featured in *Zuni Jewelry* (Bassman, 1992, p. 3). Meanwhile, Nancy Westika, Annie's daughter, helped me to identify Annie's pieces, and told me that Annie's design, in general, is not flat but slightly concave, even if the silver base is flat.

Hummingbird bracelet, channel inlay, Annie Quam Gasper, no hallmark, 1950s–60s, each medallion 0.85" across, $400–600.

Annie Quam Gasper made this Hummingbird bracelet in the channel inlay style in the 1950s or 1960s. There are four medallions on the cuff with Hummingbird designs, which are consistent with the drawing Faye Quandelacy drew for me. Each medallion measures 0.84 inches in diameter and consists of Blue Gem turquoise.

Hummingbird pin, channel inlay, Annie Quam Gasper, no hallmark, 1950s–60s, 1.31" across, $300–450.

Hummingbird ring, channel inlay, Annie Quam Gasper, no hallmark, 1950s–60s, 0.84" across, $160–240.

Hummingbird earrings, channel inlay, Annie Quam Gasper, no hallmark, 1950s–60s, 0.86" across, $200–300.

This is a matching Hummingbird ring made by Annie Quam Gasper in the channel inlay style in the 1950s or 1960s. It measures 0.85 inches in diameter.

The same artist made these Hummingbird earrings in the channel inlay style in the 1950s or 1960s. They have clip-on clasps, measure 0.86 inches in diameter, and consist of Blue Gem turquoise.

Annie Quam Gasper also made this Hummingbird pin in the 1950s or 1960s in the channel inlay style. Although it is not consistent with Faye Quandelacy's hummingbird interpretations, Nancy Westika confirms it is her mother's. It measures 1.31 inches in diameter and consists of Blue Gem Turquoise.

Hummingbird necklace, channel inlay, Ellen Quandelacy, no hallmark, 1950s–60s, central medallion 1.32" across, $600–900.

Hummingbird bolo, channel inlay, Ellen Quandelacy, no hallmark, 1940s–50s, 1.26" x 1.44", $400–600.

Hummingbird earrings, channel inlay, Ellen Quandelacy, no hallmark, 1950s–60s, 0.87" x 0.90", $200–300.

Ellen Quandelacy made this Hummingbird necklace in the channel inlay style in the 1950s or 1960s. As there is no space in the center of the design, it is consistent with the pieces in *Zuni: The Art and the People II* (Bell, 1976, p.44). The central medallion measures 1.32 inches in diameter, and the side medallions measure from 0.86 to 0.71 inches. It consists of beautiful Blue Gem turquoise.

The same artist made this Hummingbird bolo in the channel inlay style in the 1940s or 1950s. This design has two open ends and no central space. In addition, there is no inlaid stone, but silver, instead, in the two tips. It measures 1.44 inches tall and consists of Blue Gem turquoise.

These Hummingbird earrings were also made by Ellen Quandelacy in the channel inlay style in the 1940s or 1950s. This design is identical to the bolo just described, above. There are open ends and no central space in the design, and they have screw-in clasps on their backs. It measures 0.90 inches tall and consists of white mother of pearl.

Hummingbird bolo, channel inlay, Ellen Quandelacy, no hallmark, 1940s–50s, 1.32" x 1.34" across, $400–600.

Hummingbird earrings, channel inlay, Ellen Quandelacy, no hallmark, 1950s–1960s, 0.89" across, $200–300.

Hummingbird pin, channel inlay, Ellen Quandelacy, no hallmark, 1950s–60s, 1.01" across, $200–300.

Ellen Quandelacy made this Hummingbird bolo as well, in the channel inlay style in the 1940s or 1950s. This is similar to the representation of Annie's design, as drawn by Faye Quandelacy, and has an open space in the center. The central part is divided into three channels. It measures 1.34 inches tall and consists of Morenci turquoise.

These Hummingbird earrings, by Ellen Quandelacy, were made in the channel inlay style in the 1940s or 1950s. Their design is very similar to that of Annie Quam Gasper's earrings, but Ellen's has a slimmer central part. These earrings have clip-on clasps, measure 0.89 inches in diameter, and are made with Blue Gem turquoise.

In the 1950s or 1960s, Ellen Quandelacy made this Hummingbird pin in the channel inlay style. It measures 1.01 inches in diameter and is made with Blue Gem turquoise.

Hummingbird bolo, channel inlay, Ellen Quandelacy, no hallmark, 1960s, 1.33" x 1.94" across, $400–600.

This Hummingbird bolo was made by Ellen Quandelacy in the channel inlay style in the 1960s. I estimated the time of production based on the Bennett-type clasp with c-31 inscription. This is a longer version of her ordinary Hummingbird design. It measures 1.94 inches tall and consists of Fox turquoise.

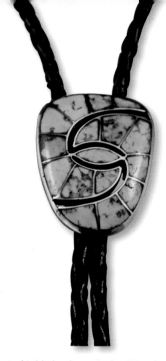

Hummingbird bolo, channel inlay, Ellen Quandelacy, no hallmark, 1950s–60s, 1.22" x1.60" across, $400–600.

The same artist made this bolo as well, in the channel inlay style in the 1950s or 1960s. It might have been made earlier than the bolo just described, above. It measures 1.60 inches tall and consists of Fox turquoise.

Rain bird bolo, channel inlay, Alice Leekya Homer, no hallmark, 1950s–60s, 1.58" x 2.26", $600–900.

Alice Leekya Homer made this Hummingbird bolo in the channel inlay style in the 1950s or 1960s. I have not seen another piece quite this one. It is a combination of a Hummingbird design and her random pattern channel inlay technique. It measures 2.26 inches tall and is made with Lone Mountain turquoise.

Mickey Mouse

and

Minnie Mouse

Mickey Mouse and Minnie Mouse designs are relatively new in Zuni jewelry. They might have been first introduced in Zuni jewelry in the 1970s, by Leo Poblano's daughter, Veronica Poblano (Nastacio), who gained fame in her early twenties. She was elected to the Arizona Highways Hall of Fame Classics in her mid-twenties, and her Mickey Mouse necklace and pin were featured in the *Hall of Fame Classics Edition* (*Arizona Highways*, August, 1974, p. 44). Her Mickey Mouse sets this design's standard. The bar is so high that no other Zuni artist has exceeded or even reached it so far. She stopped making jewelry in these designs suddenly, however, probably because of a patent problem.

Eight Rain Bird and thirteen Hummingbird pieces are included in this chapter. It is quite difficult to differentiate Frank Vacit's Rain Bird design from Dan Simplicio's, and equally challenging to distinguish Annie Gasper's and Ellen Quandelacy's Hummingbird designs from each other. Thorough research is necessary when attributing these pieces.

Minnie Mouse ring, mosaic inlay, Veronica Poblano, veronica, 1970s, 1.01" x 2.29", $300–450.

Mickey Mouse ring, mosaic inlay, Veronica Poblano, veronica, 1970s–80s, 1.09" x 2.30", $400–600.

Mickey Mouse ring, mosaic inlay, Veronica Poblano, veronica, 1970s–80s, 1.03" x 2.15", $300–450.

Veronica Poblano made this Minnie Mouse ring in the raised mosaic inlay style in the 1970s. Minnie wears a Cinderella dress. All stones and shells are three-dimensionally cut, polished, and set in the channels. This kind of three-dimensional work reminds me of her father's. It's rare that we see mosaic inlay work of such a high degree of quality. It measures 2.29 inches tall and consists of blue/green turquoise, red coral, white mother of pearl, and black jet.

The same artist made this Mickey Mouse ring in the raised mosaic inlay style in the 1970s or 1980s. Mickey's red shoes are round and smooth, and his pants are carved to show a realistic texture. One side of the ring, visible at an angle, is inlaid as well. It measures 2.30 inches tall and consists of blue turquoise, red coral, gold lip mother of pearl, white mother of pearl, and black jet.

This is another Mickey Mouse ring, also by Veronica Poblano, made in the raised mosaic inlay style in the 1970s or 1980s. He wears an orange shirt, blue pants, and red shoes. It measures 2.15 inches tall and consists of blue turquoise, red coral, orange shell, white mother of pearl, and black jet.

Mickey Mouse pin, mosaic inlay, Veronica Poblano, veronica, 1970s–80s, 0.96" x 2.16", $300–450.

Mickey Mouse ring, mosaic inlay, Veronica Poblano, veronica, 1970s–80s, 1.04" x 2.15", $300–450.

Mickey Mouse pin/pendant, mosaic inlay, Veronica Poblano, no hallmark, 1970s–80s, 1.06" x 2.13", $300–450.

Veronica Poblano made this Mickey Mouse pin/pendant as well, in the raised mosaic inlay style in the 1970s or 1980s. He wears a white shirt, orange pants, and blue shoes. It measures 2.16 inches tall and consists of blue turquoise, red coral, orange shell, white mother of pearl, and black jet.

This Mickey Mouse ring was made by the same artist, in the raised mosaic inlay style in the 1970s or 1980s. He wears a white shirt, iridescent pants, and blue shoes. He measures 2.15 inches tall and consists of blue turquoise, red coral, iridescent abalone, white mother of pearl, and black jet.

This is a Mickey Mouse pin/pendant made by Veronica Poblano in the raised mosaic inlay style in the 1970s or 1980s. He wears a violet shirt, white pants, and violet shoes. He measures 2.13 inches tall and consists of violet sugilite, purple lip mother of pearl, red coral, white mother of pearl, and black jet.

Mickey Mouse ring, mosaic inlay, Amelio Nastacio, Nastacio, 1970s, 1.02" x 2.00", $200–300.

Minnie Mouse ring, mosaic inlay, Sullivan Shebola, no hallmark, 1970s, 1.08" x 1.17", $150–225.

Mickey Mouse ring, mosaic inlay, Sullivan Shebola, no hallmark, 1970s, 1.01" x 1.09", $150–225.

This is a Mickey Mouse ring made by Amelio Nastacio in the raised mosaic style in the 1970s. It is signed "Nastacio" on its back. Mickey wears a blue shirt, gold pants, and gold shoes. He measures 2.00 inches tall and consists of blue turquoise, red coral, gold lip mother of pearl, white mother of pearl, and black jet.

Sullivan Shebola made this Minnie Mouse head ring in the raised mosaic inlay style in the 1970s. His Minnie's ribbon, compared to Veronica's, is not as three-dimensional. It measures 1.17 inches tall and consists of blue turquoise, red coral, white mother of pearl, and black jet.

The same artist made this Mickey Mouse head ring made in the raised mosaic inlay style in the 1970s. He wears a bow tie which is absent in Veronica's Mickey Mouse design. It measures 1.09 inches tall and consists of blue turquoise, red coral, white mother of pearl, and black jet.

Mickey Mouse earrings, mosaic inlay, Sullivan Shebola, no hallmark, 1970s, 1.11" x 1.17", $200–300.

These Mickey Mouse earrings were also made by Sullivan Shebola in the raised mosaic inlay style in the 1970s. Mickey wears a bow tie, and the posts from which the Mickey Mouse heads are hung are bow ties as well. Each measures 1.17 inches tall and consists of blue turquoise, red coral, white mother of pearl, and black jet.

Mickey Mouse stick pin, mosaic inlay, Carol Lasiloo, no hallmark, 1970s, 0.97" x 0.92", $150–225.

Carol Lasiloo made this Mickey Mouse stick pin in the raised mosaic inlay style in the 1970s. Her Mickey is similar to Sullivan's, except that there is neither a central turquoise part in his bow tie nor a black part in his mouth. The head measures 0.92 inches tall and consists of blue turquoise, red coral, white mother of pearl, and black jet.

Even if Mickey's and Minnie's bodies are depicted completely, it is sometimes difficult to identify the artists. It gets even more challenging if the body is absent. However, there are other minor points, we can use to identify them. First of all, we should notice their mouths: if there is a smaller black part in the mouth, it may have been made by Veronica Poblano, but, if there is a large black part, it may be Sullivan Shebola's work. Finally, if there is no black part in its mouth at all, it could be attributed to Carol Lasiloo. Needless to say, however, even in the work done in her early and mid-twenties, Veronica Poblano's design and execution are exceptional.

CONCLUSION

I have discussed almost every Zuni motif, excluding Knifewing, Rainbow Man, Sun Face, Hopi Bird, and Kachinas, as well as the Zuni artists, working mainly in the 1940s, 1950s, and 1960s, who used them. I cannot help but be amazed by the vast variety of motifs Zuni artists have made. Some motifs, such as dragonflies and antelopes, were made because of their popularity among the Zunis, while others, such as roadrunners and wagons, might have been made because of their popularity among Non-Native Americans and tourists. Other motifs, such as butterflies and eagles, were made in large quantities, as a result of their popularity on both sides of the spectrum. Some were made by many different Zuni artists, while others were made by only a select few. If a motif, such as butterfly, is made by many artists, the presence of an inter-personal variation among the pieces becomes evident. If we compare roadrunners made by Ted Edaakie

and Edward Beyuka, for example, an intra-personal variation will also be evident. These inter-personal and intra-personal variations are evidenced in my three former Zuni jewelry books, as well.

It is a certainty that, even in the 1940s, 1950s, and early 1960s, a wide variety of birds and animals were made. I usually estimate the year of production of certain bolos based on the handmade clasps on their backs. Because the first Bennett type bolo clasp was introduced in 1957, a certain bolo with a handmade silver clasp is safely assumed to have been made until the early 1960s.

As for the realistic birds and animals that Zuni artists have made, a trader told my research friend, Ernie Bulow, that Zuni artists copied anything from sources such as calendars and tobacco packages. I do not agree with this statement. Generally, Zuni artists hate to copy a design exactly, even if they borrow a motif from another medium. They almost always create their own unique designs out of the original, and they hate when others copy their designs, as well. An artist should create his or her own designs, and pursue technical perfection.

As a collector and scholar of vintage Zuni jewelry, I am anxious about the fact that Zuni jewelry Classics are sometimes copied by non-Native Americans, and artisans from other tribes and even from foreign countries. They are sometimes knock-off pieces; however, others are sometimes well-made and very difficult to judge as fakes. We have to be very careful and examine pieces thoroughly. Typically, there are one or two unnatural points in fakes. Meanwhile, Zuni artists should stamp their hallmarks on the back in addition to "Zuni, NM."

REFERENCES

Adair, John. *The Navajo and Pueblo Silversmiths*. Norman, OK: University of Oklahoma Press. 1944.

Arizona Highways. January, 1945. Phoenix: The Arizona Department of Transportation, 1945.

Arizona Highways. August, 1952. Phoenix: The Arizona Department of Transportation, 1952.

Arizona Highways. August, 1959. Phoenix: The Arizona Department of Transportation, 1959.

Arizona Highways: Hall of Fame Classics Edition. August, 1974. Phoenix: The Arizona Department of Transportation, 1974.

Bahti, Tom. *Southwestern Indian Tribes*. Las Vegas: KC Publications, 1968.

Bassman, Theda, and Michael Bassman. *Zuni Jewelry*. Atglen, PA: Schiffer Publishing, Ltd., 1992.

Baxter, Paula A. *Southwest Silver Jewelry*. Atglen, PA: Schiffer Publishing, Ltd, 2001.

Beddinger, Margery. *Indian Silver: Navajo and Pueblo Jewelers*. Albuquerque: University of New Mexico Press, 1973.

Bell, Ed, and Barbara Bell. *Zuni: The Art and the People*. Vol. 1. Grants, NM: Squaw Bell Traders, 1975.

Bell, Ed, Barbara Bell, Steve Bell, Ralph McQueary, and Jerry McQueary. *Zuni: The Art and the People*. Vol. 2. Grants, NM: Squaw Bell Traders, 1976.

Bennett, Edna Mae and John F. *Turquoise Jewelry of the Indians of the Southwest*. Colorado Springs, CO: Turquoise Books, 1973.

Bulow, Ernie. *"Mysteries of Zuni Silver: And Who Was Mingos House Anyway?"* Gallup Journey Magazine, February, 2012: 20-21.

Bulow, Ernie. *"Mysteries of Zuni Silver: Part Two."* Gallup Journey Magazine, March 2012: 20-21.

The *C. G. Wallace Auction Catalogue*. The C. G. Wallace Collection of American Indian Art. Sotheby Parke Bernet Inc., 1975.

Chalker, Kari, ed. *Totems and Turquoise: Native American Jewelry Arts of the Northwest and Southwest*. New York: Harry N. Abrams Inc., 2004.

Frank, Larry. *Indian Silver Jewelry of the Southwest: 1868-1930*. Atglen, PA: Schiffer Publishing, Ltd., 1990.

King, Dale Stuart. *Indian Silver*. Vol. 2. Tucson: Dale Stuart King, 1976.

Levy, Gordon. *Who's Who in Zuni Jewelry*. Denver: Western Arts Publishing Co., 1980.

Manley, Ray. *Photography. Ray Manley's Collecting Southwestern Indian Arts & Crafts*. Tucson: Ray Manlay Photography, Inc., 1975.

McManis, Kent. *A Guide to Zuni Fetishes and Carvings*. Tucson: Treasure Chest Books, 1995.

McManis, Kent. *Zuni Fetish Carvers: The Mid-Century Masters*. Santa Fe: The Wheelright Museum of the American Indians, 2003.

Nahohai, Milford and Elisa Phelps. *Dialogues with Zuni Potters*. Zuni, NM: Zuni Ashiwi Publishing, 1995.

Ostler, James, Rodee Marian, and Milford Nahohai. *Zuni: A Village of Silversmiths*. Zuni, NM: Zuni Ashiwi Publishing, 1996.

Schaaf, Gregory. *American Indian Jewelry*. Vol. 1. Santa Fe: CIAC Press, 2003.

Schiffer, Nancy N. *Turquoise Jewelry*. Atglen, PA: Schiffer Publishing, Ltd., 1990.

Schiffer, Nancy N. *Jewelry by Southwest American Indians: Evolving Designs*. Atglen, PA: Schiffer Publishing, Ltd., 1990.

Sei, Toshio. *Knifewing and Rainbow Man in Zuni Jewelry*. Atglen, PA: Schiffer Publishing, Ltd., 2010.

Sei, Toshio. *Hopi Bird and Sun Face in Zuni Jewelry*. Atglen, PA: Schiffer Publishing, Ltd., 2011.

Slaney, Deborah C. *Blue Gem, White Metal: Carvings and Jewelry from the C. G. Wallace Collection*. Phoenix: Heard Museum, 1998.

Wright, Barton, and William Harmsen. *Patterns and Sources of Zuni Kachinas*. Denver: Harmsen Publishing, 1988.

INDEX